The Opinionated Knitter
Elizabeth Zimmermann
Newsletters 1958 - 1968

Models:

Cecilia, Liesl and Renata Monroy

Katherine Olson

Lloie Schwartz

Cully, Eli and Michelle Wolfe Swansen

Photography and book design, Meg Swansen

Photograph on page 123 & cover by T. S. Zimmermann

Publishing Assistant, Michelle Wolfe

Technical Editor, Lizbeth Upitis

Proofreader, Tami Schiferl

Overall Assistant, Eleanor Haase

Original instructions and stories, Elizabeth Zimmermann

Additional text, Meg Swansen

©2005 Schoolhouse Press

Fifth printing, 2008

Schoolhouse Press

Pittsville, WI 54466

(715)884-2799

www.schoolhousepress.com

ISBN-10: 0-942018-26-5

ISBN-13: 978-0-942018-26-4

Library of Congress Control Number : 2004097260

Nearly all the wools used for the garments in this book were
supplied by Schoolhouse Press. We will be pleased to send you a
catalogue upon request, or visit our website:

www.schoolhousepress.com

Printed in the USA

Table of Contents

Newsletters

#1. Fair Isle Yoke Sweater — page 10

    EPS, Yoke schematic — page 15

#2. Scandinavian Sweaters (2) — page 16

#3. Graphs for Knitting Color-Patterns — page 22

    EPS, Dropped Shoulder schematic — page 25

#4. Classic "Brooks" Saddle-shoulder — page 26

#5. Sheepsdown; four garments — page 30

#6. Aran Sweater or Cardigan — page 36

#7. Tomten Jacket — page 42

#8. Seamless Raglan Sweater — page 48

#9. Garter-Stitch Blanket — page 52

#10. Woodsman's Socks — page 56

#11. Five Caps (2) — page 58

#12. V-Necked Aran Cardigan — page 66

#13. Three & One Sweater — page 72

#14. Icelandic Yoke Sweater — page 76

#15. Mittens — page 80

#16. Eight Unusual Knitting Techniques — page 84

#17. Leggings (adult and baby) — page 88

#18. Stockings — page 90

#19. Spiral Hat — page 94

#20. Kangaroo Pouch Sweater — page 98

#21. Baby Surprise Jacket — page 102

#22. Bonnet, Bootees, Bunting — page 108

and . . .

Adult Surprise Jacket — page 112

Wool Gathering #62 — page 120

plus . . .

from notebooks and journals, *Elizabeth writes:*

very brief biography — page 5

cross-country skiing — page 7

history of Wool Gathering — page 8

dropped stitches — page 16

excerpts from tv series' — pages 20, 21

Mother's Day — page 27

German Christmas — pages 36, 37

Canadian journal — pages 38 - 41

Aran knitting — page 70

at the Schoolhouse — page 77

Easter — page 83

biographical notes — pages 86, 87

journal — pages 91 + 118, 119

black bread — pages 108, 109

spectacles — page 115

Many of the garments in this book were sent to us by knitters from around the country.
"knitted by..." credit is shown in each photograph, except the endpapers. Listed alphabetically, the contributors are:

Rollie Abkowitz	Betty Kendrick	Becky Skidmore
Alison Albrecht	Carol Knott	Joy Slayton
Kevin Ames	Jean Krebs	Judith Sopher
Carol Anderson	Jane Lippmann	Meg Swansen
Mary Anderson	Dale Long	Sue Wallace
Janine Bajus	Linda Lutz	Jinny Lee Waters
Renate Baur	Maxene Mollen	Elaine Wedeking
Greg Cotton	Holly Nieding	Joyce Williams
Joan Debolt	Jackie Ritchie	Andrea Wong
Nancy Ellingson	Barbara Rottman	Lois Young
Judy Franklin	Joan Schrouder	Diane Zangl
Eleanor Haase	Ann Seybold	Elizabeth Zimmermann
Therese Inverso	Lloie Schwartz	

books by Elizabeth Zimmermann
- Knitting Without Tears (Simon & Schuster) - KWT
- Knitter's Almanac (Dover Publications) - KA
- Knitting Workshop (Schoolhouse Press) - EZKW
- Knitting Around (Schoolhouse Press) - KAR

Videos with Elizabeth Zimmermann
- Knitting Workshop (6 hours, 3 cassettes)
- Knitting Glossary (4 hours, 2 cassettes or DVD)
- Knitting Around (6 hours, 3 cassettes)

Audio Tape of Elizabeth
reading *Digressions* from her book, Knitting Around

Schoolhouse Press titles - in published order

Knitting Workshop	Elizabeth Zimmermann	Latvian Mittens	Lizbeth Upitis
The Tale of Alain	Arnold E. Zimmermann	Mosaic Knitting*	Barbara G. Walker
Catalog	Arnold E. Zimmermann	A Treasury of Knitting Patterns	Barbara G. Walker
Knitting Around	Elizabeth Zimmermann	A Second Treasury of Knitting Patterns	Barbara G. Walker
The Lonely Lake	Arnold E. Zimmermann	Charted Knitting Designs	Barbara G. Walker
Barbara Abbey's Knitting Lace	Barbara Abbey	Latvian Dreams	Joyce Williams
Notes on Double Knitting*	Beverly Royce	A Fourth Treasury of Knitting Patterns	Barbara G. Walker
Designs for Knitting Kilt Hose*	Veronica Gainford	Sweaters From Camp	Knitting Campers
Handknitting With Meg Swansen	Meg Swansen	Unexpected Knitting	Debbie New
Knitting From the Top	Barbara G. Walker	Two-End Knitting	Anne-Maj Ling
The Kitchen Table Cookbook*	Lloie Schwartz	The Kitchen Table Recipe Book	Lloie Schwartz
Knitting Languages*	Margaret Heathman	A House Filled with Music	Margret Rettich
Faroese Knitting Patterns	Marilyn van Keppel		
Learn-to-Knit Afghan Book	Barbara G. Walker		

out-of-print

When Elizabeth died in November of 1999, the New York Times wrote an unusually long obituary, complete with her photograph and a schematic of EPS. The Times described Elizabeth as, "... a woman who brought a penetrating intellect and a sculptor's sensitivity to revolutionizing the ancient art of knitting."

Here, as written to the British guild, Slip Knot, is a very brief synopsis of her life:

May 10, 1988
In answer to your request, here are some biographical details:
Born 1910 in London (Maida Vale) to Grace (née Greenwood) and Herbert Lloyd-Jones.
Childhood mainly in Birchington, Kent and Brightlingsee, Essex.
School: Oaklea*, (then in Essex), Art school in Lausanne, Switzerland and then the Akademie in München, Bavaria.
In 1937 married Arnold Zimmermann (who didn't like Hitler, nor Hitler him), in Wealdstone Registry Office and then off! to the U.S., where brewmasters were needed. Arnold is a good one. We lived on Long Island NY, in New Hope PA, Milwaukee WI and now in the northern part of that state.
Three kids, Thomas, Lloie and Meg.
When Arnold retired we moved to our dear old abandoned brick schoolhouse bang in the middle of rural Wisconsin where we've lived happily now for 20 years or so.
I love to knit and had many of my designs accepted by several publications. Discovered some splendid unbleached wool and started a small mail-order knitting-book-and wool business thirty years ago. (NO synthetics.)
Started to disagree with printed knitting directions as too primitive or too complicated, so began putting out one-page leaflets of my own (later to blossom into our twelve-page Wool Gathering).
Increasing age and mail order knitting business started to grate on each other, so passed the whole works on to our daughter, Meg Swansen, who runs it with great success.
We started Knitting Camp in 1974 which draws knitters from across the US to enthusiastic weeks at the local branch of the University of Wisconsin.
Dear me; all the above reads utterly boastful. But true.

*Just yesterday I found the following in the Oaklea alumni newsletter, Old Girls' League: "Betty Lloyd-Jones - Elizabeth Zimmermann. In December last year, Betty wrote: *'I am a full-blown U.S. citizen and achieved this honour during World War Two when I was – having married a citizen of Munich – actually German. (Generous people, the Americans.) We have three American kids and two ditto grandchildren, and live happily in the wilds of Central Wisconsin in a rescued and converted old one-room brick schoolhouse. My main interest is handknitting and I well remember making a yellow-and-white jumper at Oaklea, under the watchful eye of Miss Ben.'*"

The original Newsletters, typos and all, are presented on the following pages. Occasionally Elizabeth revised the first version slightly for a reprint and, if there are significant differences, we will show you both old and new. Additional text by me, Meg.

You will see a few black and white snapshots interspersed through the pages; they are from the '70s when our kids were little. It was only upon designing the layout that some of the new photos of my grandchildren reminded me of old snapshots.

The Opinionated Knitter is a name by which Elizabeth referred to herself *(see page 8)*, and was the title she wanted to use for her first book – but Scribner's chose Knitting Without Tears, instead. We seize this opportunity to, at last, accede to her wish.

Knit on, with confidence and hope, through all crises.

Elizabeth.

Elizabeth writes: 1972. How long before my skiing days are over?

Last year I thought I was through. It was a fairly snowless winter and we were very busy, so my beautiful Swedish cross-country skis gazed at me reproachfully and untouched.

As a young woman I considered myself competent on skis, having been lucky enough to have enjoyed about a decade of Alpine skiing. Standards were gentle in those days. Snappy turns on a well-groomed slope were considered more meretricious than otherwise and the main attributes of a good skier were endurance, strong legs and a love of discomfort - richly rewarded by breath-taking descents through virgin snow. Lifts were for the rich and worldly. Alcohol and aprés-ski?: as Miss Brodie so truly said, "For people who like that sort of thing, that is the sort of thing they like."

... But I do enjoy skiing; the smell of the wax, the effort of getting the bindings just so, the slipping of hands into mittens and mittens into pole-straps, the first few happy thumps of skis on good powder snow; all these take me back to my youth, which memory tells me was carefree, but which reason tells me was nothing of the kind.

When the Old Man made me a present, therefore, of some very beautiful cross-country skis, I was pleased and grateful. ... Competently equipped, then, we make dreamlike trips through our own river-bottoms, which are terra incognita most of the year because of mosquitoes, floods and generally soggy conditions.

It is inexpressibly beautiful to glide through the snowy woods, making our own trails and seeing only the other trails of winged or four-legged creatures, busy on their own affairs. We skim along, softly up, softly down.

Sometimes we pack a little lunch so that we can go further afield and take advantage of the short winter day. Our dinner table was once a three inch slab of ice, firmly frozen to a tree trunk and stuck there when the swollen but frozen river returned to its normal level.

I shall never be an expert, but at least I can keep up with the Old Man when his pace is moderate. Just the right form of exercise for an Old Woman.

Our skis are beautiful in themselves. Mine are blue, with the royal Swedish emblem; the Old Man's came to the U.S. with us thirty-five years ago, after many years of racing and honorable service in the Alps. He bought them off a guy in Norway where they had been made by Marius Eriksson, Sr who got his hickory from Amerika; so they have returned to the land of their beginnings. For several years they were used only in Forest Park just beyond Brooklyn; later they served him on the rolling hills of Bucks County, PA and then in the Kettle Moraine near Milwaukee.

When we return home, good-night all; under the featherbed for a luxurious afternoon nap. What fun it is to be an old lady, honourably entitled to the likes of this. The book slips from the hand, the eyes close, I'll count to eleven ... five, six, seven ... nothing more. Out like a light.

End of seasonable digression.

The history of Newsletter *(NL)* and Wool Gathering *(WG)*, from Elizabeth's Journal #2.
P.S. When *WG* are sold out, we reprint the instructions onto a single-sheet Spun Out *(SO)*

Feb 1st. Monday
I took a week off to wrestle with WG. This has happened semi-annually now for 14 years and it looks as if it will go on as long as there is breath in my body. From year to year it becomes more rewarding.

Back in 1957 when my Wool Trade was in its infancy I started a newsletter. The first two were long skinny sheets with various items of woolly interest: in which magazines my designs had appeared, which wools to use for what, etc.

Then in 1958 my heart was once again broken by the publishing of one of my designs with some most inferior, not to say misleading directions. Magazine editors frequently impose their own knitting theories upon the helpless freelancer. So I said to myself, dammit, I'll put out my own directions in my own newsletter, free to wool customers, 25¢ to everyone else. And Newsletter #1 appeared. It is still in existence in its original form and has a certain archaic, if not to say amateurish, aspect with a very wasteful layout. It was well received and was followed by numbers 2 through 22. Eleven years, My Word! I realized that I was sending out thousands for free, at great cost in money and time. In fact about 1/6 of the year was consumed by Newsletter and a change in tactics was called for. I decided to up the price 300% and cut the free list drastically. At least my husband and children decided for me - I was still yammering about "too expensive" and "customer good will". But the family was right. Nobody even blinked at the price-increase; some even said they welcomed it as they had felt that only paying a quarter, or even nothing, had been like taking candy from a baby. Me.

Of course by charging more, I could afford to shift from one single large sheet to two large sheets, printed on both sides and folded.

With more space at my command I could give more detailed and discursive directions which I have found that knitters like. Too long have we knitters scratched along on the meagre diet of conventional "directions", abbreviated, condensed and whittled down generally to allow more space for the photographs. Being my own "editor" and headily independent, I dispense with photographs entirely, contenting myself with amateurish but accurate drawings. Expert draughtsmen are not usually knitters and I feel I can convey my own ideas clearly and succinctly, though without slickness. And as for photographs - nothing dates so fast as -- not the sweaters necessarily -- but the models.

Our minds were a blank as to a title (although I hankered then as now, to be known as **The Opinionated Knitter***) so I started a small contest with a prize, and this brought forth the truly inspired suggestion of "Wool Gathering". So Wool Gathering it is and will remain - my means of expression, my pulpit, my soapbox.*

Paradoxically, now that I have more space, I find it easier to fill and to my increasing surprise, I receive few rebuttals to my frequently unorthodox whims and theories.

So there is the history of Newsletter/Wool Gathering. My husband says the foregoing is like a commercial, but it was not so intended. I fondly hope it to be of general interest and exemplary of the fact that if you really have something to say about which you feel strongly, some of the people will listen some of the time.

Elizabeth Zimmermann

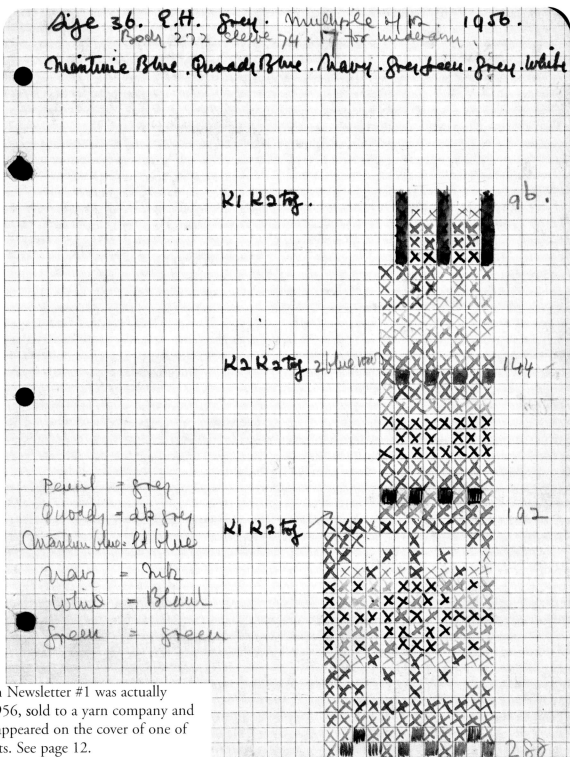

The sweater in Newsletter #1 was actually designed in 1956, sold to a yarn company and subsequently appeared on the cover of one of their pamphlets. See page 12.

The color names are those of the old one-strand Homespun Wool Elizabeth used for the prototype; Shetland Wool yields the same gauge.

Elizabeth Zimmermann

ELIZABETH ZIMMERMANN
2010 EAST WOOD PLACE
MILWAUKEE 11, WISCONSIN

Price 25¢
Leaflet #1

FAIRISLE YOKE SWEATER MADE ENTIRELY ON CIRCULAR NEEDLES.   GAUGE 6 st to 1".

Materials. 8 oz Shetland or 3 skeins "Homespun" for main colour.
     1 oz of each of four harmonizing colours for yoke.
1 24" circular needle #2 for welt.(This may also be worked on straight needles and sewn up)
 1 24" circular needle #4, or any size to give above gauge, for body and lower yoke.
1 set sock needles #2, for cuffs and neck edge.
1 16" circular needle #4, or any size to give above gauge, for sleeves and upper yoke.

Measurements of completed sweater. Bust 36". Overall length from back of neck 23".
     Sleeve length and body length to underarm, as
desired. For each extra inch of width desired, add 6 st to body.

Body. With #2 needle(s) cast on 200 st. K 2, P 2, firmly for 30 rows. Change to
     larger needle, and increase evenly to 212 st. Work in stocking st until piece
measures 15" or desired length. Place 18 st at each underarm on thread or holder(X)

Sleeve. With size 2 sock needles cast on 48 st. K 2, P 2, for 30 rows. Change to
     16" needle and increase evenly to 60 st. Work in stocking st until piece
measures 8". Increase 2 st at underarm, and repeat this every 1½" until there are
74 st. Work even until piece measures 22" or desired length to underarm. Place
18 st at underarm on thread or holder.(X) Make second sleeve to correspond.

Yoke. Place all 288 st of body and sleeves on larger 24" circular needle, matching
     underarms, (X) and work around for 8 rows. Work pattern A. Next round,
K 1, K 2 tog, all around. Work pattern B, changing to 16" needle if indicated.
Next round, K 2, K 2 tog, all around. Work pattern C. Next round, K 1, K 2 tog,
all around. There should be about 96 st, or anyway a multiple of 4. Work 1 round
in main colour and change to #2 sock needles, and shape neck as follows:-

Neck. K 2, P 2, over 48 st of back of neck. Turn. Work in K 2, P 2, over 50 st.
     Turn. Work in K 2, P 2, over 52 st. Turn. Continue in this way until 6 rows
have been completed, then work around for a further 7 rows. Bind off loosely. Weave
together at underarms. Run double thread of nylon elastic around neck and adjust to fit.

Newsletter #1 was mailed in **September 1958** and Elizabeth gingerly imported a small amount of wool from the Shetland Islands to support the design.

Consider employing a number of the tricks Elizabeth devised since this design was initially published:
- Phoney Seams on body and sleeves.
- Short Rows across the back of the body.
- Mirror-image sleeve increases each side of three center underarm stitches.
- With three decrease rounds in the yoke, the initial reduction is quite severe and can result in puckering. I have altered the three decreases from 1/3 each time to
     1/4 (k2, k2tog)
     1/3 (k1, k2tog)
     2/5 (k2, k2tog, k2tog) You will end up with the same number of neck stitches; 40% of the body stitches.
 - Or, for a large-circumference sweater, I use four decrease rounds instead of three.
     1/5 (k3, k2tog) around
     1/4 (k2, k2tog) around
     1/4 (k2, k2tog) around
     1/3 (k1, k2tog) around

schematic on page 15

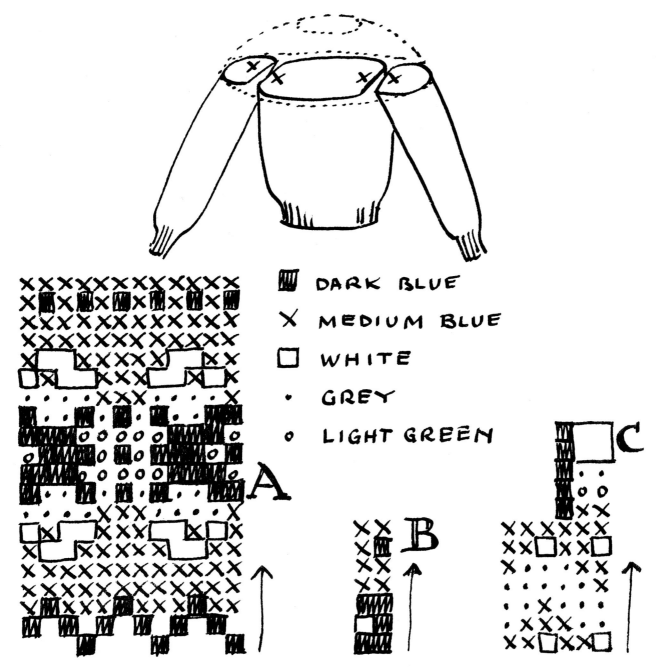

DARK BLUE
MEDIUM BLUE
WHITE
GREY
LIGHT GREEN

Cast on and cast off loosely.
Be sure to work at the correct GAUGE.
When knitting colour patterns, carry the yarn loosely across the back of your work.

- Instead of all the neck shaping at the top of the yoke, consider working 2 or 3 sets of Short Rows at the base of the yoke, right after joining in the sleeves (these short rows will begin and end about 10-12 stitches into the front yoke; much further forward than you may imagine), then 2 or 3 more sets of short rows at the yoke top, as written above.

12

By the late '50s, Elizabeth was becoming established as a designer with her patterns appearing regularly in *Vogue Knitting, McCall's* and *Woman's Day* magazines, as well as some yarn-company pamphlets from *Pauline Denham, Spinnerin, Bernat* and *Unger*.

This Fair Isle Yoke sweater had appeared on the cover of a yarn company's school-and-college issue, with flat pieces substituted for Elizabeth's seamless instructions. Her disappointment was keen and it was then that she decided to write, print and edit her own patterns. Thus, *Newsletter #1* was produced and mailed in September of 1958.

Sweater styles at the time were slim-fitting; have since swung to voluminous and now, in 2004, are veering back to body-hugging. Using Elizabeth's Percentage System (EPS) you can adjust all the dimensions to suit current fashion and/or your own taste and achieve a perfect fit.

See the EPS-Yoke schematic on page 15.

knitted by Sue Wallace

knitted by Betty Kendrick

knitted by Nancy Ellingson

Elizabeth Zimmermann

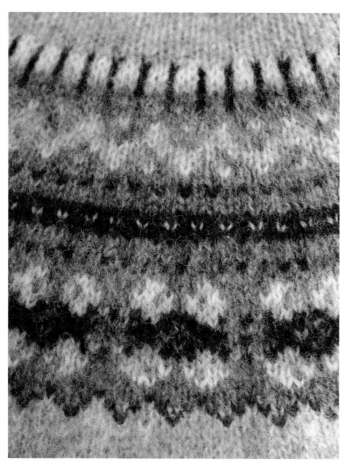

Here are the colors Elizabeth used for the cover-sweater
mentioned on the opposite page. Knitted by Therese Inverso.

Six more possible color combinations knitted by Joyce Williams.
All sweaters (except Sue Wallace's) and swatches were knitted in pure Shetland wool.

Elizabeth's simple percentage system (which her son-in-law, Chris, named EPS) is a means by which you can make a custom fitted, seamless sweater by multiplying *your* gauge times wanted body circumference. The resulting number equals 100%, or the Key Number [K]. Other sweater measurements will be a percentage of [K].

The percentages gradually declared themselves to Elizabeth through the scores of seamless sweaters she had knitted over many years and she began to get a handle on the concept as early as 1959; see Newsletter #2 on page 17.

In the '50's and '60's, sweaters were quite slim fitting and Elizabeth's original design called for a 33% of [K] upper sleeve. The yoke was then shaped with three concentric rings of decreases; getting rid of 1/3 of the number of stitches on the needle during each of the three decrease rounds (k1, k2tog around).

After having knitted a number of yoke sweaters, I was displeased with the slight puckering that sometimes resulted from the initial decrease. Since I always knitted with wool I could block the yoke smooth, but in the late 1970s it occurred to me to reduce the severity of the first decrease from 1/3 to 1/4 (k2, k2tog around). In order still to arrive at an approximately 40% neck opening, that meant the second decrease would be 1/3 (but on fewer stitches, thus eliminating any gathers) and the final decrease had to be 2/5 (k1, k2tog, k2tog around) ... quite a severe decrease, but on relatively few stitches and the garment is then travelling horizontally across the shoulders.

The above worked well until I began knitting larger sizes and increased the upper sleeve to about 35 - 40% of [K] instead of 33%. As Medrith Glover discovered, the yoke - measured vertically - is rarely greater than 10-11" deep, regardless of body girth. That means, for a large garment, you have the same vertical space in which to decrease more stitches. To cope with that, I added another decrease-ring and made the first decrease 1/5 of the number of stitches on the needle: k3, k2tog around ... nice and relaxed... followed by 1/4, 1/4 and 1/3 (see schematic on opposite page).

The seamless yoke style is constructed by knitting the body from lower edge to underarm, then knitting the sleeves from cuff to underarm. Put 8-10% of [K] underarm stitches on a thread and knit the sleeves onto the body. After uniting the three sections you are at a crossroads and can work the seamless yoke section in any of a number of different styles:

- Saddle-Shoulder *(see pages 4-7)*
- Raglan *(see pages 48-51)*
- Shirt-Yoke *(see EZKW)*
- Hybrid *(see EZKW)*
- Set-In Sleeve *(see EZKW or SO# 21)*
- Circle garter-stitch yoke *(see WG#33 or SO #38)*
- Basket weave/Entrelac *(see WG#32 or SO#31)*
- Box-the-Compass *(see WG#31 or MSK)*
- Lap-Shoulder*(see WG#5 or SO#28)*
- Yoke variations *(WG#65, SO# 2, 4, 5, 7, 17, 24)*

Except for The Nalgar, they all begin in the same manner:
- Body-to-underarm -
- Sleeves-to-underarm -
- UNITE ...

which, Patience Boyd observed, sounds rather like a rallying call.

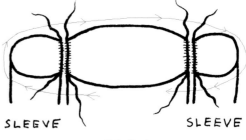

SLEEVE SLEEVE

BODY

If you are making an oversized sweater with 40% upper sleeves, there may remain more than 40% stitches by the time you reach wanted yoke depth. Plan to add a ribbed neck border, as you can then hide a severe decrease in the first ribbed round by working K2, P2tog, P1 (or K1, P2tog) as many times as needed.

All of the above-listed styles are available in Elizabeth's publications. Some, like the raglan and the saddle shoulder, are classic; others are Elizabeth's (and my) original designs.

I will always feel gratitude to the knitter who once said to Elizabeth, in a challenging tone, "Well! You can't knit a Set-In Sleeve in the round."

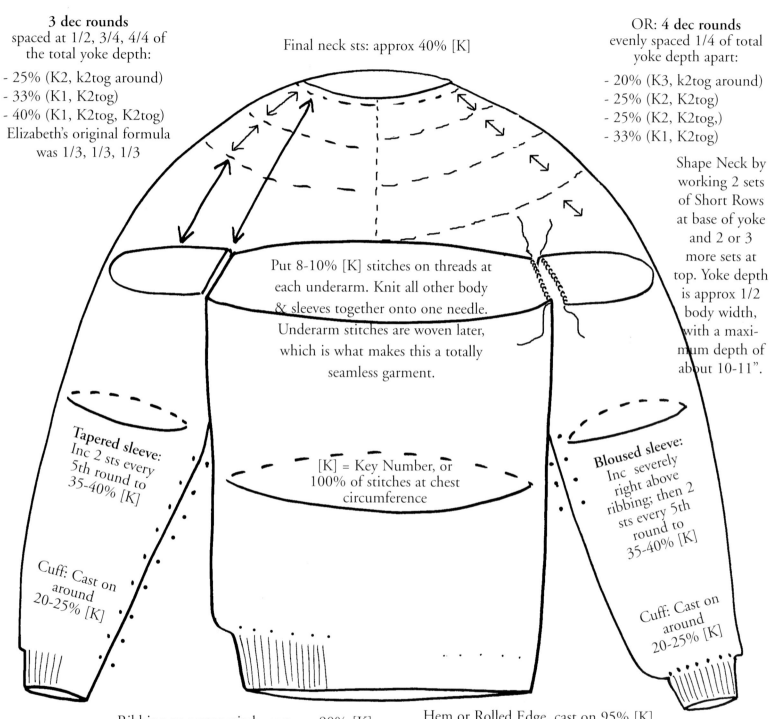

3 dec rounds
spaced at 1/2, 3/4, 4/4 of the total yoke depth:

- 25% (K2, k2tog around)
- 33% (K1, K2tog)
- 40% (K1, K2tog, K2tog)
Elizabeth's original formula was 1/3, 1/3, 1/3

Final neck sts: approx 40% [K]

OR: **4 dec rounds**
evenly spaced 1/4 of total yoke depth apart:

- 20% (K3, k2tog around)
- 25% (K2, K2tog)
- 25% (K2, K2tog,)
- 33% (K1, K2tog)

Shape Neck by working 2 sets of Short Rows at base of yoke and 2 or 3 more sets at top. Yoke depth is approx 1/2 body width, with a maximum depth of about 10-11".

Put 8-10% [K] stitches on threads at each underarm. Knit all other body & sleeves together onto one needle. Underarm stitches are woven later, which is what makes this a totally seamless garment.

Tapered sleeve:
Inc 2 sts every 5th round to 35-40% [K]

Cuff: Cast on around 20-25% [K]

[K] = Key Number, or 100% of stitches at chest circumference

Bloused sleeve:
Inc severely right above ribbing; then 2 sts every 5th round to 35-40% [K]

Cuff: Cast on around 20-25% [K]

Ribbing or garter-stitch, cast on 90% [K]. Inc to 100% in first round above lower edge.

Hem or Rolled Edge, cast on 95% [K]. Increase to 100% above rolled edge - or in pairs at side "seams" as you work up the body

Elizabeth Zimmermann

MILWAUKEE 11, WISCONSIN
ELIZABETH ZIMMERMANN
2010 EAST WOOD PLACE

Price 25¢
Leaflet #2

HOW TO DESIGN AND MAKE A SCANDINAVIAN SKI-SWEATER

MATERIALS. (for a size 38 sweater approximately)
    5-6 skeins 2-ply Sheepswool or 7-8 skeins Fisherman Yarn(5 st to 1"). Average sweater.
    6-7 skeins 3-ply Sheepswool (4 st to 1"). Heavy sweater.
    7-8 skeins 4-ply Sheepswool (3½ or even 3 st to 1"). Extremely heavy sweater.
Proportions should be about 1/3 of pattern colour and 2/3 of background colour. Be sure to order enough . I will always take back unopened skeins. You will need 1 24" circular needle and 1 16" circular needle of a size to give the above gauges. Also 1 set of sock needles and 1 24" circular needle two sizes smaller if you are ribbing bottom and cuffs.

DESIGN. The classic ski-sweater has almost no shaping, being a straight tube for the body, with straight cuts for the armholes. The sleeves are narrower tubes, widened at the underarms by knitted-in gussets.

GAUGE. This is MOST IMPORTANT. The fit of your sweater depends on it. Knit a swatch of at least 3" X 3" in stocking st, (K 1 row, P 1 row),with the needle you plan to use. Steam it gently and measure how many st there are to 1". Varying your needle if necessary, try to achieve the above gauges, according to which yarn you are using.

SIZE. Decide how wide you want the sweater to be -- usually about chest measurement plus 3" or 4", and multiply this by your gauge. You now have the amount of st needed for the body. This is the only measurement you will need to start with.

START KNITTING. For a hem at the bottom, on the 24" needle cast on 10 st less than you have calculated. Join, being careful not to twist, and K around for 1½" to 2". Increase 10 st evenly spaced around. P 1 row, and continue in knitting. After 2 rounds begin pattern, using any of the patterns from p.2, and having 2-3 rows background colour in between. Use alternate wide and narrow patterns if you wish, or make the lower part in snowflakes with patterns across chest and shoulders. Carry one colour in one hand, and one in the other, knitting the "German" and the "American" way alternately. This may take some practice, but it is worth it, and your yarns will not be twisted if you have to unravel -- which God forbid. None of these patterns have more than 5 straight st of one colour, so twisting is unnecessary. Carry yarn VERY loosely across back of work. A loose thread can always be tightened later, but a tightly-knitted pattern spoils your sweater. Change patterns at the same point each time.

Elizabeth writes:

If stitches slip off the needle, keep calm. Slip them on again. ... This brings us to the second -- or lifetime -- position of knitted stitches. While the stitch is on the needle, it stands sideways with the righthand side towards you and in front of the needle; the other or lefthand side away from you on the back of the needle. But as soon as the stitch of the next round has been pulled through it, it turns smartly to the left and stands there, facing the audience until the end of time, the brave little thing.

STOP KNITTING at shoulder height. Bind off.

SLEEVES. Start at the top by casting on half the amount of body st on 16" needle. Work in
    pattern, using different designs from the body if you wish, and decrease 2 st at
underarm every 2nd row for gusset. When sleeve is desired width continue working straight
to desired length to cuff, finishing with a hem as on body, or with 30 rows K2, P2, on
smaller needles.

MAKING UP. Mark the armholes to match the top of sleeves by running a basting thread. Stitch
    with small machine-stitch and fairly loose tension twice each side of basting, and cut
on basting line. Sew up 1/3 of top of body for each shoulder, leaving 1/3 for neck. Lap
tops of sleeves over armholes and hem neatly in place from right side. Press the inside
edges towards sleeves and neaten on the inside with herring-bone st.
Pick up around neck and finish with one more pattern and a hem, or
with ribbing. Run wide (pyjama) elastic through bottom if desired.

IF YOU WISH TO MAKE A CARDIGAN, stitch and cut down
    the front as you did for the armholes, and
also cut out a scoop for the neck front, (about 6"
across and 2½" deep.) Pick up st along edge --
2 st for every 3 rows -- and work a few rows in
ribbing or garter st, making 3-st buttonholes
down one side. Or finish with ribbon.

VARIATIONS IN COLOUR AND DESIGN ARE ENDLESS. You
    can make the hems in bright and unexpected
colours, or use a different colour for the last
few rows of body and the first few rows of
sleeves. Hunt up old designs in cross-stitch
books, or use names and initials or club
insignia. Vary your colours as you please, but
don't carry more than two at once. It isn't worth it.

Mailed in Sept 1959.
You can see Elizabeth's editing above, in preparation for the revised edition of this Newsletter shown on the next two pages.

I consider this a relatively historic document because of the instruction to cast on 1/5 of the number of body stitches for the cuff ... here, in 1959, is the rudimentary beginning of EPS.

Over the years, many other designers have used Elizabeth's percentage system and most of them have been very generous about giving credit to the originator.

Elizabeth Zimmermann

ELIZABETH ZIMMERMANN
BOX 157
BABCOCK, WISCONSIN 54413

Leaflet # **2** from Spring 1959
Scandinavian ski-sweater. 25¢
Second, and, it is to be hoped,
improved edition. Winter 1968.
reprinted 1982

<u>ONE-OF-A-KIND SCANDINAVIAN SWEATERS. DESIGN AND MAKE YOUR OWN ON CIRCULAR NEEDLES.</u>

<u>MATERIALS</u> for a sweater 40" around, approximately 27" long.
6-7 skeins 2-ply Sheepswool...5 sts. to 1"...Medium weight sweater.
7-8 skeins Fisherman Yarn.....5 sts. to 1"... "   "   "
7-8 skeins 3-ply Sheepswool...4 sts. to 1"...Heavy sweater.
6-7 wheels Icelandic doubled..4 sts. to 1"...Heavy, lovely, and unusual sweater.
8-9 skeins 4-ply Sheepswool...3½sts. to 1"...Very heavy sweater.
8-9 skeins Sheepsdown.........3 sts. to 1"...Extra thick, but not too heavy sweater.
One 24" and one 16" needle(circular) of a size to give you the above GAUGES.
(Approx. sizes 5-10½). My needles are exchangeable if in original package.
Yarn proportions are about 1/3 pattern-colour and 2/3 background-colour. Dyelots
vary; be sure to order plenty. I will always take back unopened skeins.

<u>DESIGN</u>: This is where you make your sweater your own. Pick colours that please
and suit you. Use traditional designs given here, or those in leaflet #3. You
may of course use designs from any source, or, best of all, invent your own. This
is not difficult; take squared paper and experiment. There are only two rules:-
1. Never carry more than 2 colours at one time; mistrust(or change)such designs.
2. Never plan for more than 5 consecutive horizontal sts. of one colour. Fill in
large spaces with small stars, flowerets, or whatnot. Sometimes a single stitch is
enough. A classic ski-sweater has almost no shaping, being a straight tube for the
body, with straight cuts for armholes. Sleeves are narrower tubes, gently tapered
from wrist to armhole. Shoulders are dropped, so sleeves are relatively short.
Use shirtsleeve length for measurement from back-of-neck to wrist.

<u>SIZE</u>: MAKE A SWATCH 30 sts. wide and 3-4" long. Count the number of sts. to 3" and
divide by 3. The result is <u>your</u> GAUGE; don't be even ¼ stitch off! Decide how
wide you want your sweater by measuring <u>your</u> favourite old one, or yourself at
your widest. Multiply this width by your GAUGE, and the result is the number of
stitches to cast on. Men are a different shape; start for them with hip measure-
-ment, and taper out. 2 sts. increased at sideseams every 4-5" is usually enough.

<u>START KNITTING</u>: With 24" needle, cast on the amount of sts. you have calculated.
Join, being very careful not to twist, mark 1st st. carefully, and K around for 2-3
rnds. Now start putting in patterns, always starting at 1st st., and changing each
pattern-rnd. at exactly this point. There will be a small unavoidable muddle here,
but it will be at underarm seam, and won't show. Carry one colour in one hand, and
one in the other, working the "German" and "English" way alternately. This will
take practice, but is worth it. You will gain surprising speed, and yarns will not
twist. It is not necessary to twist yarns which are carried for 5 sts. or less.

The dots to the left of each motif chart indicate, Repeat.

Centre large patterns, back and front. You need not centre small patterns of 4-st
repeat or less. Carry yarn very loosely across back of work. Loose threads may be
tightened later, but a tight neat "carry" will pucker, and ruin your sweater.
To follow graphs, work from R to L. Repeat when you reach the dot, and work one rnd
Change to second line of graph at first st. of next rnd. If you wish, make a plain
sweater with patterns just across the shoulders. You may alternate patterns, or
repeat a single one, or make a "Sampler Sweater", with as many patterns as possible.
Work as many plain rnds between patterns as you think look good.

STOP KNITTING at shoulder height; 27", or desired length. You may shape shoulder-
-backs by working back and forth on back only, leaving 5 sts. behind every row until
you have about 1/3 of back-sts. left. Work around on all sts, and cast off firmly.

SLEEVES: Start at wrist on 16" needle. Cast on 20%(1/5)of body sts. very loosely,
so sts. will go around needle, or use sock-needles until you have about 50 sts. Work
in pattern, using different ones from body if you wish. Inc. 2 sts. at underarms
every 4th rnd, keeping increases strictly vertical, and fitting in pattern-sts.
When sleeve is right length (17-18" approx.) to join dropped shoulder, cast off.
Don't make sleeves too long; sleeve plus ½ body equals shirtlseeve length.

MAKING UP: Mark armhole to match exactly the top of sleeve by running a basting
thread. Stitch twice each side of basting with small machine-st. and loose tension.
Cut on basting. Sew up about 1/3 of body for each shoulder. Lap tops of sleeves
over armholes and hem neatly from right side, "holding in" the armhole. Press
inside edges towards sleeve and neaten with herring-bone st. Pick up all sts. at
lower edges, with right side towards you. P 1 rnd, K 1 rnd, next rnd, K2, K2 tog
around(10% decr). Work for 1½-2". Don't cast off, but sew down elastically,
taking one st. for each knit st. Pick up all sts around neck, work one small pattern, and finish with similar hem. Or make a turtle-neck of K2, P2 ribbing. For a
flat turned-under hem, inc. 2 sts each side every rnd.
(at neck)

REMEMBER, this is your sweater; don't necessarily copy anything or anybody.

Good Knitting — Elizabeth.

Because very few knitters knit and purl at the exact same tension, we do not recommend a flat swatch for circular projects.
Instead, knit a **Swatch Cap:** Cast On about 90 stitches and
work a bit of garter-stitch or ribbing to prevent the lower
edge from curling. Now increase to around 110 stitches and
begin to work some of the color patterns. When the Swatch
Cap is about 4-5 inches deep, you can steam it, take a gauge
reading and either finish the cap or begin your sweater.

Or, knit a **Speed Swatch:** With a circular needle, cast on
about 40 stitches and work a few ridges of garter stitch (back
and forth) to prevent curling. Add the second color and *knit
across the 40 stitches. Slide the stitches back around the
circle, so that the first stitch is again at the tip of the left
needle. Pull out long strands of both colors, loop them across
the back and repeat from *. Continue until you have about 5
inches. If you are not pleased with the look and feel of the
knitting, shift your needle size up or down and knit some
more until you like the result. Steam-block the swatch and
take a reading (stay a few stitches in from the distorted
selvedges). Since you have only knitted with the "right" side
facing, you have a flat, circular swatch.

Tip: Work first and last stitch of each row with both
colors together to keep edges as tidy as possible.

knitted by Elizabeth Zimmermann

This design may also be found in Chapter 3 of Elizabeth's book, Knitting Without Tears; but it was first seen on her second television series for PBS: The Busy Knitter 2 in 1967. Although both series were stored in the PBS vaults in Washington D.C, they had been recorded on relatively primitive tape, suffered severe drop-out damage and were destroyed a number of years ago.

The first PBS program in 1966, The Busy Knitter, was a 10-week series that covered all details for knitting a circular, seamless Raglan pullover or cardigan, which was introduced by Elizabeth as follows:

This is Elizabeth Zimmermann, the Busy Knitter. I propose, during the next ten sessions, to guide you through the apparent intricacies of a classic raglan sweater or cardigan, seamless, purl-less and made entirely on circular needles. I think, when we are through, you will agree that there are few knitting problems that will not yield to a blend of common sense, ingenuity and resourcefulness; that working on your project has been simple and pleasurable and that you have achieved a handsome, comfortable garment that will FIT.

The program was so popular that PBS requested a second one. Elizabeth had found the original title rather dull and wanted to liven things up a bit by calling the second series, *The Busy Knitter Rides Again.* The decision-makers at the station were not amused and it was called *The Busy Knitter 2.*

The sweater on this page is the original one Elizabeth knitted for the second series. On the opposite page is a version knitted by Sue Wallace -- lengthened by inserting an additional large motif.

In the PBS instruction booklet for The Busy Knitter 2, Elizabeth wrote:

... this time we will knit a ski sweater of Scandinavian type: straight body, straight armholes and sleeve-tops and slightly tapered sleeves. We can thus concentrate our full attention on the design and execution of the color patterns.

My sweater will be of 3-ply Sheepswool* in cream (background) and dark oatmeal (patterns), as this is typical of many of the lovely old sweaters made before bleaching and dyeing were common. It will be worked at a GAUGE of 4 stitches to 1" on 160 stitches and will thus be 40" around...

I do not urge that you reproduce my sweater exactly. On the contrary, it will give me pleasure to imagine many of you working out your sweaters in individual colors and designs. ...

If at all possible, buy the best yarn, which is not necessarily the most expensive!

And at the end of the booklet:

Knitting is a most ancient skill and I like to think that it was done even before weaving, since the tools are so basic and simple. Two sticks and a piece of thread and you can begin. It enables you to make warm, comfortable garments with few or no seams if you wish. It is soothing to do and can be carried everywhere with you. It offers endless possibilities of design and is a craft medium which is only now starting to be re-explored."

*Please note that Sheepswool was re-designed by the mill several decades ago and is now thicker than it used to be. This sweater will be quite heavy in 3-ply, but knits up beautifully in 2-ply at about 4-1/4 to 4-1/2 sts to 1". Also, you may combine 2-ply natural Sheepswool with the rich, dyed colors of Rangeley Wool if you wish, as they are identical weights.

knitted by Sue Wallace

Elizabeth Zimmermann

ELIZABETH ZIMMERMANN
BOX 5555   MILWAUKEE, WIS. 53211

Leaflet #3   1968.
Graphs for knitting
colour-patterns.25¢.

These patterns have been carefully chosen as suitable for colour-pattern knitting.
They have been gathered from many sources; #8,9,13,16 and 27 are my own. As you will
see, they call for carrying yarn for a maximum of 5 sts -- often not even that much.
Work from Right to Left, starting with bottom line. At dot, repeat around (or across)
your project. Change pattern-rnds strictly at first st of every rnd. Vary colours as
you wish, but never work with more than two at one time. Hold one colour in either
hand, working the right-handed and the left-handed way alternately, i.e. knit one
colour the way you are acustomed to knit, and the other colour the way some other
people knit. It will be slow at first, but with practice you will speed up astonish-
-ingly. One important admonition -- carry yarn very loosely across the back of your
work, otherwise your knitting will pucker, and be wasted and unloved.

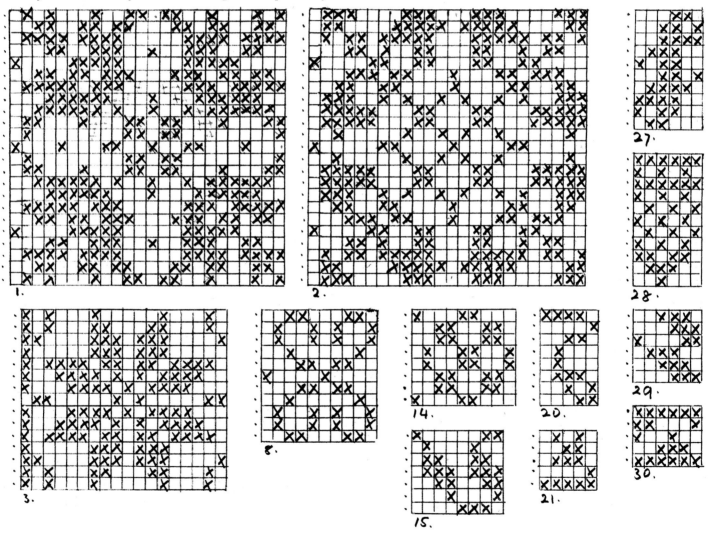

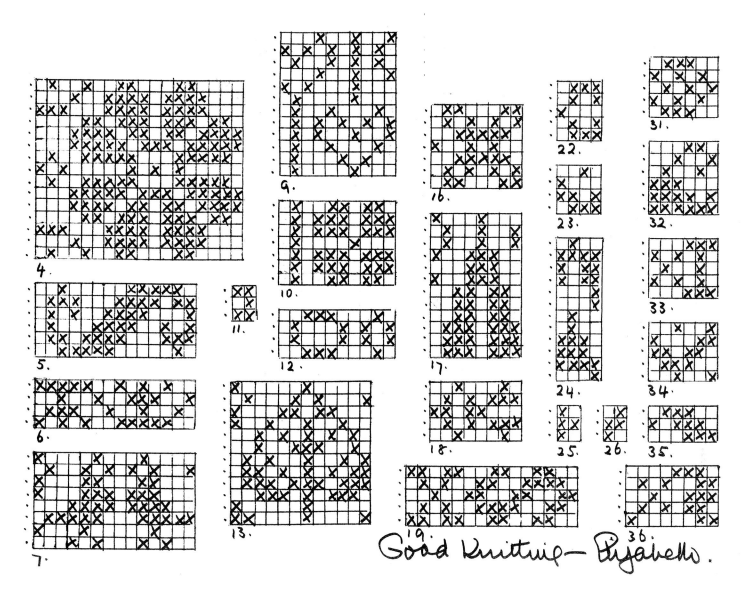

4. 5. 6. 7. 9. 10. 11. 12. 13. 16. 17. 18. 19. 22. 23. 24. 25. 26. 31. 32. 33. 34. 35. 36.

Good Knitting — Elizabeth.

When working color-patterns, it is advisable to keep the carried color loops fairly short across the back of the work, as rings and fingers can easily snag and pucker the fabric; or worse, break the strand.

Elizabeth's rule of thumb was not to carry a strand across more than 5 stitches (see NL#2 on page 18). If presented, for instance, with an eleven-stitch stretch, Elizabeth would add a "snowflake" in the middle of that carry and break it into five - one - five. Or twist/trap the two colors around each other in the middle of the carry.

My guideline varies slightly: instead of five-stitches, I will carry for one inch without trapping. However, some instructions will ask you to trap the carried wool every two or three stitches, thus producing a very dense fabric. As always, Knitter's Choice.

Whenever possible, trap the carried color above a stitch of the same color or tone. Then, even if you get the dreaded peeking-through, the little blip will not be noticed.

knitted by Joyce Williams

Elizabeth Zimmermann

Straight-Drop (L side), or Modified Drop-Shoulder (R side) using Elizabeth's Percentage System (EPS)

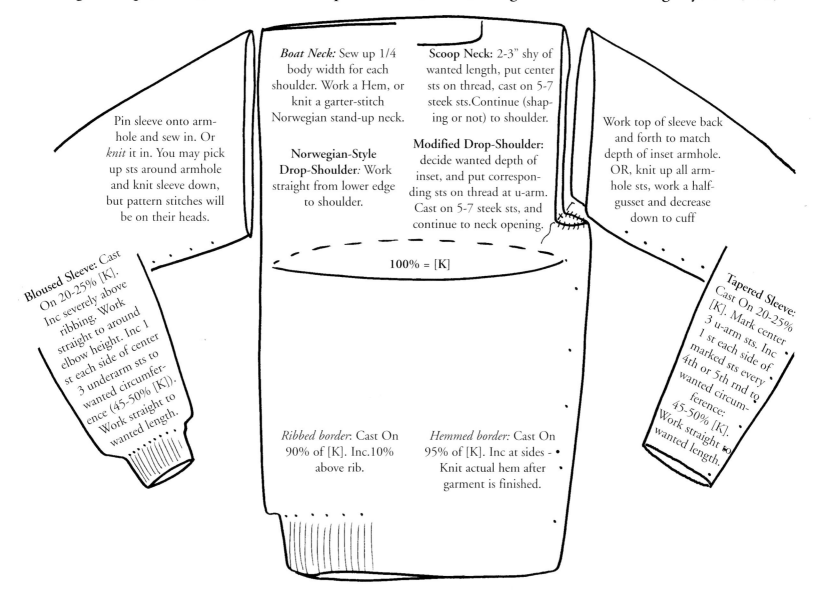

Boat Neck: Sew up 1/4 body width for each shoulder. Work a Hem, or knit a garter-stitch Norwegian stand-up neck.

Norwegian-Style Drop-Shoulder: Work straight from lower edge to shoulder.

Pin sleeve onto armhole and sew in. Or *knit* it in. You may pick up sts around armhole and knit sleeve down, but pattern stitches will be on their heads.

Scoop Neck: 2-3" shy of wanted length, put center sts on thread, cast on 5-7 steek sts.Continue (shaping or not) to shoulder.

Modified Drop-Shoulder: decide wanted depth of inset, and put corresponding sts on thread at u-arm. Cast on 5-7 steek sts, and continue to neck opening.

Work top of sleeve back and forth to match depth of inset armhole. OR, knit up all armhole sts, work a half-gusset and decrease down to cuff

Bloused Sleeve: Cast On 20-25% [K]. Inc severely above ribbing. Work straight to around elbow height. Inc 1 st each side of center 3 underarm sts to wanted circumference (45-50% [K]). Work straight to wanted length.

Tapered Sleeve: Cast On 20-25% [K]. Mark center 3 u-arm sts. Inc 1 st each side of marked sts every 4th or 5th rnd to wanted circumference: 45-50% [K]. Work straight to wanted length.

100% = [K]

Ribbed border: Cast On 90% of [K]. Inc.10% above rib.

Hemmed border: Cast On 95% of [K]. Inc at sides - Knit actual hem after garment is finished.

For a cardigan, allow 5-7 extra Cast On (steek) stitches at the center front as a field for the future cutting. Stitch (or crochet) and cut center front as for armholes. The cardigan border may be knitted all in one piece, directly onto the cut edge.

To provide comfort and ease for the wearer, consider adding underarm gussets: 3-4 inches shy of the underarm, increase each side of 1 or 3 side "seam" stitches every 3rd or 4th round to about 4-5" wide. Put gusset stitches on a thread and cast on 5-7 steek stitches. Reverse the above for top-down sleeves, or match the above for cuff-up sleeves.

The neck shape may be anything you like: do nothing for a straight boatneck -- but the resulting high neck-front may annoy the wearer. Consider a **square neck:** put about 8-9" worth of center-front stitches on a thread when you reach the base of your proposed neck. Cast on 5-7 steek stitches and continue to shoulder. For a **scooped neck:** put about 5-6" worth of stitches on a thread, make a steek and decrease away the additional width by k2tog, knit steek, ssk every round or every-other round, depending upon the shape you want. For a **V-neck,** put 3 sts on a coil-less pin and shape on each side every 2nd, 3rd or 4th round (depending upon what angle you want) to wanted width; then straight to wanted height.

Elizabeth Zimmermann

ELIZABETH ZIMMERMANN
BOX 5555 MILWAUKEE, WIS. 53211

Leaflet #**4**, from Spring 1960   25¢.
Classic "Brooks" sweater.
Second, and, it is to hoped, improved
Edition.   Winter 1965.

Dear Knitter,

          Here is a new way to make an old favourite -- a classic "Brooks" sweater with
epaulet (or saddle) shoulders. It is worked from the bottom up entirely on circular needles.
Body and sleeves are made separately to the armholes; then all but the underarm stitches are
put on one needle, and decreased up to the neck in facsimile of set-in sleeves with epaulet
shoulders. Lastly, the underarm seams are woven together, and lo, a seamless garment results.

The number of stitches to cast on depends on your own measurements and on the GAUGE of your
knitting. GAUGE means the number of stitches to 1". To determine GAUGE, make a swatch* in
stocking-stitch, 24 sts. wide and 3" long, with the yarn and needles you plan to use. Block
by steaming gently, and count the number of sts. to 3". Divide this by 3 to ensure obtaining
an average inch. Multiply the GAUGE by the number of inches around your sweater, & the result
is the number of sts. to cast on. Below are directions for a useful 40" sweater at a GAUGE of
5 sts. to 1". I used a #5 needle, but you may knit more tightly or loosely than I do, and need
a larger or smaller needle respectively. <u>Please</u> check your GAUGE strictly before you start.
Figures in parentheses serve as a percentage guide if you have more or less than 200 sts.

<u>CIRCULAR SEAMLESS "BROOKS" SWEATER</u>. 40" around, 23" long.
<u>GAUGE</u>. 5 sts to 1".
<u>MATERIALS</u>. 4 skeins "Homespun", <u>or</u> 5 skeins 2-ply Sheepswool, <u>or</u>
     6 skeins Fisherman Yarn. Amounts are generous; unused skeins
always may be returned. 1 24" and 1 16" circular needle, of a size
to give <u>you</u> 5 sts. to 1". Maybe 4 sock-needles for lower sleeves.
<u>BODY</u>. With 24" needle, cast on 200 sts. Join, being careful not to
     twist, and K for 14½". (Borders are worked later). Put 16 sts.
(8% of 200 sts of body) on thread at each underarm. Set aside.
<u>SLEEVE</u>. With 4 needles cast on 40 sts. (20% of 200). Join, and work
     around, increasing 2 sts. at underarm every 5th rnd. Soon you
will have enough sts for the 16" needle. At 66 sts. (approx. 33% of
200) work straight until sleeve measures 18", or desired length to
underarm, allowing for border. Work another sleeve. Put all sts. of
body and sleeves on 24" needle, matching underarms, (see diagram),
and work straight for 2".
<u>SHOULDER SHAPING</u>. Measure your own shoulder-width, (in my case 14").
     Multiply this by your GAUGE, and the result -- 70 sts. (35% of
200)-- is the amount of sts. for front and back. Place markers (I
prefer safety-pins; they don't have to be moved every row), 70 sts.
apart on front and back. Remaining sts. are for sleeves, and should
be equal on both sides. Now:- Work across front to 1st marker, sl 1,
K 1, psso (pass slipped st over). Work across R sleeve to within
2 sts. of 2nd marker, K 2 tog. Work across back to 3rd marker, sl 1,
K 1, psso. Work across L sleeve to within 2 sts of 4th marker, K 2
tog. You have thus decreased 4 sts. in 1 rnd. Rep this rnd. until
16 sts. (8% of 200) remain on each sleeve. Now:- Change the direc-
-tion of your decreases by knitting 2 tog. where you have been doing
sl 1, K 1, psso, and vice versa, always keeping intact the 16 sts.

of sleeves. Do this for 10 rnds, and then make epaulets:- K 15 sts.
of R sleeve, sl 1, K 1, psso. Turn. P 15, P 2 tog. Turn. Rep. these
two little rows until approx ¼ of shoulder-width (18 sts) has been
decreased on R side. Work across to L sleeve and repeat. There
should be approx. 34 sts. left on front and on back. Work back and
forth on the 34 sts of back, decreasing 1 st off epaulets at the
end of each row, as you did for shoulders. After 16 rows you will

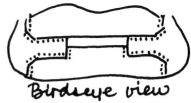

Birdseye view

have consumed half the epaulets. All that remains to be done is to work around on all
remaining sts. for about 1" in ribbing or garter-st. Cast off loosely, and run elastic
thread through inside of neck-edge, adjusting to fit. Weave underarms. Pick up all sts.
around lower edge. P 1 rnd, K 1 rnd. Decr 10% (K 8, K 2 tog. around), and work a good inch
for hem. Do not cast off, but turn in and sew up with neat loose stitches, one for each K st.
Finish cuffs in the same way. Edges may be finished in garter-st, also on 10% less sts. Or
you may have begun with 30 rnds. of K 2, P 2, ribbing, but hems have superseded this for the
time being, and I, for one, am glad.
<u>FOR 3/4 SLEEVES</u>. Cast on 50 sts, (25% of 200). Work as for long sleeves, but stop at 12".
<u>FOR A CARDIGAN</u>. Before working neck-edge, baste down centre front. With small stitch and
    loose tension, machine-st. twice each side of basting. Cut on basting. Pick up at the
rate of 2 sts. for every 3 rows up R front, K around neck, and pick up down L front. Work a
border in garter-st, mitering neck-front by increasing 2 sts. at this point every 2nd row.
If your sweater is a little narrow, make a wide border. If it has turned out much too big
cut out a strip down the front. Make 7 buttonholes ½" in from the edge on both sides, so that
sweater may pass freely back and forth from son to daughter, by changing buttons. Trim the
fuzz off the cut edges, press flat, and neaten on the inside with matching thread.

*A swatch is not wasted labour by any means;
it makes an excellent pocket..

Happy Knitting — Elizabeth.

knitted by Elizabeth Zimmermann

Elizabeth writes:
*I deplore Mother's Day. Mother has it good and if anyone loves her
and wants to show it, one measly day in the year is a pretty
squinchy space of time in which to do it.*

A knitter writes,
"*Knitter's Almanac* is my favorite book of all time! I have a
degree in literature. I read constantly. I own thousands of books.
My husband says I own EVERY knitting book ever published
(he might be right). And, still, if I were going to a deserted
island and could take only one book -- *Knitter's Almanac!*"

L knitted by Barbara Rottman   R knitted by Janine Bajus

Elizabeth Zimmermann

knitted by Meg Swansen

The Opinionated Knitter

Newsletter & Leaflet #5.   Fall 1960.
Free to all current customers. Extra copies 25¢.

ELIZABETH ZIMMERMANN
BOX 5555 -:- MILWAUKEE 11, WISCONSIN

Dear Knitter,
          S H E E P S D O W N . . . , the name is a paradox, but you must admit
that it is descriptive. It is the happy result of collaboration between the
Sheepswool mill and me, to satisfy demand for a yarn to knit Cowichan Indian
sweaters in a lighter, smoother, less pungent form. Keep design and shape
simple, and let the material work for you. It's a natural for Christmas
presents, as it works up so fast. The final texture is light and fleecy,
and ineffably warm and thick. Make allowance for this thickness (actually $\frac{1}{2}$"
in colour patterns), and make your sweater wider than usual, to leave room for the
wearer inside.... Though tough when knitted, Sheepsdown has not great tensile
strength, so work it with a light hand, and tell me if you want some matching
yarn (free) for sewing up.

For COWICHAN SWEATER use my leaflet #2, and a gauge of $2\frac{1}{2}$ st or 3 st to 1"
on a $10\frac{1}{2}$ circular needle. Add a shawl collar,(A), which is just a 6"-wide
strip of garter-st, sewn on afterwards.

But there is another possibility for Sheepsdown in "Prime Rib" stitch,
which goes as follows:-
Row 1. *K 1, yarn fwd, sl next st as if to P, bring yarn back over
R needle, repeat from *.
Row 2. K 1, *yarn fwd, sl next st as if to P. bring yarn back over
R needle, K 2 tog, rep. from *. Rep. row 2 for pattern. This is a very
w-i-d-e stitch, so allow for it. 36 st give a width of about 23".....
All right, then, PRIME RIB SWEATER (B) takes 7-8 skeins Sheepsdown
for an average size (23" across, 24" long). With #15 needles, make
a swatch. Multiply the number of st to 1" (about $1\frac{1}{2}$...) by desired
width. Cast on resulting number of st, and work 4" - 5" on smaller
needles. Change to #15 needles and work straight to desired length to
shoulder. Cast off 1/3 for each shoulder, and continue on centre 1/3 to
desired length for collar. Cast off loosely. Back and front are the
same. For sleeve, start at top with $\frac{1}{2}$ the amount of body st. Work to
desired length to cuff, decreasing 1 st each side every 2" (about 10 rows).
Cast off. Sew up shoulders and collar. Sew in sleeves. Sew up underarm
and sleeve seams. That's it. (I always sew from the right side; it's neater.

The striped Sheepsdown Watch Cap shown on page 34 and
64 was knitted decades ago as I toyed with color possibilities
in this Brioche stitch that Elizabeth named "Prime Rib", and
is worked as follows:

    Using a 16" circular needle, cast on in Color A (from 32
to 36 stitches) of thick Sheepsdown and work Prime Rib
across all stitches, according to the above instructions. Turn,
and, with Color B, * work across. When you have knitted the
last stitch, slide the stitches around the 16" needle so you
have access to the first stitch of that row and WRAP it as
follows: slip the first stitch, bring the working wool forward,
replace the slipped stitch and turn. Pick up color A. and
work across, wrap, turn, change color. Repeat from *,
switching colors after each row. Because of the wrap, you will
be "sewing" up the seam as you knit. Nice.

    At present, the Watch Cap may take more than one skein.
If you do not want the hat to turn up at the bottom, you may
be able to squeeze it out of a single skein; see page 53.

Elizabeth Zimmermann

Then there is the ARAN COAT, (C), which may be any length you please;
8-12 skeins Sheepsdown. Use same directions and needle as for Cowich-
-an sweater, but leave out colour patterns, substituting any Aran
patterns or cables that please you. At shoulder height, cast off 1/3
for each shoulder, and continue on centre 1/3 with 16" circular needle
for hood. (12"-14")✗ Cast off. Make sleeves according to leaflet #2.
Cut armholes to match sleeve-tops. Cut centre front. Sew up shoulders
and hood-top. From right side, pick up st around front, taking 2 st
for every 3 rows. Work 8-10 rows garter-st, putting in buttonholes if
desired, and cast off on wrong side. Frog fastenings look good, or you
can put in a zipper. Sew in sleeves, and neaten cut edges on inside.
May be lined with jersey✗ Inc 2 st at centre back every 2nd row for 3"-4".

How about a NORSE SWEATER? (D) Again use leaflet #2, but in stocking st
until the upper 4"-5" of body, when you let loose with any elaborate
stitch or colour-pattern that takes your fancy. For additional colours,
Fisherman Yarn doubled is fine. End with 3-4 rnds of the darkest colour, and repeat the
same patterns for tops of sleeves. The dark colour joining at right angles is good.

Lastly, the WATCH CAP, (E), which my husband calls Tamerlane, my daughters très Dior,
and which my son and I just wear for warmth. With #11 needles work 10" in
Prime Rib, then 4 rows in K1, P1 rib. Next row, sl 1, K 1, psso, across.
P 1 row, K 1 row, P 1 row. Thread yarn through st, and draw tight. Sew up.
Try on. Isn't it beautiful? Everyone will wear it a different way; boys,
girls, and parents. I can make one in well under 2 hrs with one skein
Sheepsdown. Nice evening's work.

Well, there you have S H E E P S D O W N. Now you are on your own.
Please let me know how you like it, if you have suggestions, or if you
need help. I deliberately keep my knitting notes vague, because tastes
vary, and your brains are as good as mine anyway. But I have had experience,
and am always glad to help with knotty problems if I can. For stitch-by-stitch
directions, the stores are awash with "Books".

Special note to Wisconsin knitters. Three of my sweaters - all in Sheepsdown - will be in the 40th
Annual Exhibition of Wisconsin Crafts at the Memorial Art Center in Milwaukee, Nov 3rd - Dec 11th.

Stop Press. I believe and hope that there will be two of my sweaters in Woman's Day for Nov. '60.
I call them the Old Tow-Rope, and the More-than-Oriental-Splendour. See if you can spot them. The
former is in 3-ply Sheepswool, the latter in Fisherman Yarn and 2-ply Sheepswool.

Oh yes, and for people with access to the Canadian edition of Winter 1960-61 McCall's Needlework,
the woman's sweater on p. 80-1 is one of mine. Fisherman Yarn.

Sincerely

Elizabeth

knitted by Elizabeth Zimmermann

above: Elizabeth's grandson, Cully, swathed in Sheepsdown scarf, hat and Tomten. The scarf is just a strip of Prime Rib stitch with a few inches of K1, P1 at each end to prevent flare; the hat and Tomten are on pages 31 and 42 respectively; all knitted by his ma. Caption on a similar postcard-photo: "Life would be so much easier if only mother would stop knitting."

The shot reminds me of Ralphie's little brother in Jean Shepherd's "A Christmas Story".

left: the Prime Rib Sweater.

opposite: the dark Aran coat is the prototype that Elizabeth knitted in 1960 to celebrate Sheepsdown. Decades later, I knitted the pale grey version, which has a Set-In Sleeve Saddle Shoulder plus Snow Cuffs. Both versions have EZ's After-Thought Pockets *(see page 114)*, hoods, wide garter-stitch front borders and twisted-loop buttonholes.

E l i z a b e t h   Z i m m e r m a n n

knitted by Meg Swansen

knitted by Elizabeth Zimmermann

The Opinionated Knitter

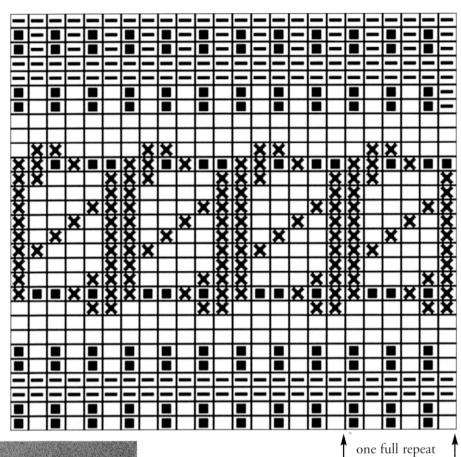

= red

= cream

= black

= oatmeal

Elizabeth added
occasional purl
stitches in both the
cream motif and the
red accents; the black
stripe is purled on
the second round.

one full repeat

Hat, sweater and mittens knitted by Elizabeth Zimmermann

knitted by Meg Swansen

E l i z a b e t h   Z i m m e r m a n n

Elizabeth tried to find a commercial equivalent to the beautiful, thick, hand-spun wool used for traditional Cowichan sweaters -- to no avail. So she went to the Cambridge Woollen Mill, from whom she already obtained 2- and 3-ply Sheepswool, to ask the owner, Ed Bjorklund, to try to duplicate a skein of handspun she had. After considerable trial and error, Mr. Bjorklund came up with this beautiful, thick, gently-spun four-ply, undyed wool which Elizabeth named *Sheepsdown*. In this Newsletter, she designed a number of garments specifically suited to her new wool.

Instructions for the striped hat shown opposite are on pages 30 - 31.

Elizabeth named the sweater shown here, SIWASH, which, if you trace the main motif with your finger, is a word you **could** write from those squiggles. The pattern chart is shown opposite.

Sheepsdown was (and still is) available in four natural undyed shades and Elizabeth doubled the bright red and black Canadian Québécoise wool to match the weight of Sheepsdown.

knitted by Elizabeth Zimmermann

Elizabeth Zimmermann

ELIZABETH ZIMMERMANN

BOX 5555 MILWAUKEE, WIS. 53211

Leaflet #6, from Spring 1961
Circular Aran sweater or cardigan.
Second, and, it is to be hoped,
improved edition.   Fall 1965

Dear Knitter,
          Having decided that I greatly prefer making Aran sweaters on circular needles, I think
you may like to know how I do it. I keep the shape as simple as possible, making a straight tube
for the body, and tapered tubes for sleeves. Armholes are straight, with dropped shoulders. The
body should be loose; a useful size is about 42" around, and directions below are for this width.
I take ¼ of this - 10½" - and work out a pattern-sequence to fit. This will be repeated 4 times
around the sweater. For a cardigan, cut down front. I shall not ask you to make the hated swatch,
but a useful cap, which will familiarize you with the patterns, and give you a perfect GAUGE.

<u>GAUGE.</u> 5 sts to 1", measured over stocking-stitch.

<u>MATERIALS.</u> 5 skeins 2-ply Sheepswool in Cream or Oatmeal.
     1 16" and 1 24" circular needle of a size to give <u>you</u>
the above GAUGE. I knit loosely, and take #5. 1 set of
4 sock-needles for lower sleeves.

<u>CAP.</u> With 16" needle cast on 108 sts. Join, and P 1 rnd.
     Now establish patterns, starting with rnd 1 in each:-
K4, P2, Blackberry, P2, Ribbon Cable, P3, Sheepfold, P3,
Ribbon Cable, P2, Blackberry, P2. You are halfway around
your cap. Rep the foregoing. Position of designs is now
established. Follow each one separately. You will find
that Things Happen every 6th rnd; in between you can re-
-lax. After 6-8" you will long to start the sweater, so
shape cap to a point by decreasing 4 times somewhere on
every rnd. When 4 sts remain, fasten off. Cap may be
none too clean, so block by washing. Measure. If cap is
narrower than half desired sweater-width, add a few P sts
between patterns; if wider, take a few out. Or widen or
narrow the K4 rib. Remember, 5 sts gives you 1"

<u>SWEATER BODY.</u> With 24" needle, cast on 216 sts for 42".
     Establish pattern-sequence 4 times. Work straight to
shoulder. Cast off. K4 ribs are at centre-front and
-back, and at sides, giving the completed garment a nice
foldline. They are also guides for cutting armholes and
centre-front. You may slope the shoulder-backs a little
or shape neck-front, in each case over 36 sts, or 1/6 of
total width.

<u>BLACKBERRY.</u> 3 sts. 6 rnds.
*<u>Rnds 1 through 5.</u> K into
back of st(Kl b),Pl, Kl b.
<u>Rnd 6.</u>Kl b, K into front,
back, front, back and front
of next st (5 sts), turn,
K5, turn, K5, turn, K5, sl
2nd, 3rd, 4th, and 5th sts
over lst st, K into back of
lst st, Kl b. Blackberry
completed. Repeat from *.

<u>RIBBON CABLE.</u>9 sts. 12 rnds.
*<u>Rnds 1 through 5.</u> K9.
<u>Rnd 6.</u> sl 2 sts on spare
needle and hold in front of
work, K2, K2 from spare
needle,(R over L 4st cable),
Kl, sl 2 sts on spare needle
and hold in back of work,K2,
K2 from spare needle (L over
R 4st cable).
<u>Rnds 7 through 11.</u> K9.
<u>Rnd 12.</u> L over R 4st cable,
Kl, R over L 4st cable.
Rep from *.

Elizabeth writes:

I am influenced by my memory of a German Christmas -- at least Christmas in Bavaria and Austria. There, people get Santa Claus out of their hair on December 6th with the feast of Saint Nikolaus, who officially inaugurates the Holy season at the

beginning of Advent. After Nikolaus there is still plenty of time for present-making, cookie-baking and all the preparations which are, let's face it, the best and most satisfying part of Christmas.

SLEEVES. Start at lower edge with 44 sts on 4 needles.
(When width permits, change to 16" needle.) Arrange
patterns as you like. I had Sheepfold up the middle,
flanked by Ribbon Cable, and all other sts in P, except
for a K4 line at underarm. Inc 1 st each side of this
rib every 6th rnd. This ties in nicely with your busy
rnds. For a roomier armhole, inc. every 5th rnd, or even
every 4th rnd. When sleeve plus ¼ body width equals
shirtsleeve length, cast off. Don't make sleeves too
long -- remember the dropped shoulders.

MAKING-UP. Mark armholes to match sleeve-tops by running
a basting-thread. Stitch with small machine-st twice
each side of basting. Cut on basting-line. Sew up approx
1/3 of top for each shoulder. Lap tops of sleeves over
armholes and hem neatly in place from right side. Press
inside edges towards sleeves and neaten with herringbone
st. For turtle-neck, with 16" needle pick up all sts
around neck and work 1-2" in rib or garter-st. For cardi-
-gan, machine st and cut out neck-front and down centre-
-front. With 24" needle, pick up 2 sts for every 3 rows
up R front (K around neck) and down L front. Work 12
rows garter-st, making 3-st buttonholes as desired. For
mitred corner at neck-front, inc 2 sts at this point
every 2nd rnd. Cast off in P on right side, working
tightly across the back of the neck.

This sweater is admittedly ornate, like many true Arans.
Originally the distinctive patterns belonged strictly to
certain families. Ribbon Cable and Blackberries are trad-
-itional, but Sheepfold is my own invention. Natural un-
-bleached wool has a high lanolin-content, and is water-
resistant until after a few washings; cleaning removes it immediately. If you use the Oatmeal-
coloured wool it will need washing very rarely, indeed, for though you know it must be dirty,
it won't look it.

Happy Knitting - Elizabeth.

SHEEPFOLD. 12 sts. 24 rnds.
*1. K 2nd st from back,
    K 1st st, sl both sts
    off L needle together.
    (B twist), K8, K 2nd st
    from front, K 1st st, sl
    both sts off L needle
    together (F twist).
2. P1, B tw, K6, F tw, K1.
3. P2, B tw, K4, F tw, K2.
4. P3, B tw, K2, F tw, K3.
5. P4, B tw, F tw, K4.
6. P5, F tw, K5.
7. P4, F tw, K6.
8. P3, F tw, K7.
9. P2, F tw, K8.
10. P1, F tw, K9.
11. F tw, K10.
12. K12.
13. B tw, K8, F tw.
14. K1, B tw, K6, F tw, P1.
15. K2, B tw, K4, F tw, P2.
16. K3, B tw, K2, F tw, P3.
17. K4, B tw, F tw, P4.
18. K5, B tw, P5.
19. K6, B tw, P4.
20. K7, B tw, P3.
21. K8, B tw, P2.
22. K9, B tw, P1.
23. K10, B tw.
24. K12. Rep from *.

IMPORTANT NOTE. The above
directions are for
CIRCULAR NEEDLES ONLY.

The high point of the South German Christmas is early evening on December 24th, preceding the actual (celebrated) birth of the Christchild. Sanna (sic) and his sack of loot are not even mentioned -- he had his day three weeks ago with a big bag of good things left on the doorstep or windowsill -- it is the Christchild who brings the presents, and they are opened in the parlour at five in the evening; one present at a time so that each one is enjoyed by the whole family. Everybody is dressed in their best and the tree is alive and alight with candles, cookies, fruit and tinsel.

A festive meal will follow after which the children tumble exhausted into bed. The adults can finish off the evening in peace and contentment and go to a beautiful midnight Mass if such is their will.

knitted by Jinny Lee Waters and Diane Zangl

The following was written with a pale blue felt-tip pen in one of Elizabeth's journals (see page 40).

She and my father – Gaffer, or The Old Man – were on their annual camping trip to Canada with their Siamese cat, KLINE (always written in all caps). Their practice was to drive until the road turned to a logging track and eventually ended altogether at the water's edge; pack all camping gear into their canoe, head out to a remote island and see no other people for two weeks.

The Camp Jacket Elizabeth refers to is a version of her Modular Tomten design; Lloie is wearing it on page 46.

Mon. Sept 27 1971. It writes! 2 years ago we left this island; today we came to it again. No one had been here in between. Firewood was still stacked by the fireplace we had built, and a bundle of kindling rolled in a plastic bag had become wet because the bag had been torn: perhaps by mice? On top of it lay, as an offering to the island, the light blue felt tip pen which had run quite dry when I was scribbling away at KWT (Knitting Without Tears). *Today it writes again and I feel as if I had come full circle. The book it timidly but enthusiastically wrote is published and I'm embarked on this, its successor.* The light blue pen, by writing again, links them.*

We have never camped so late in the year and anticipate considerable cold, damp and discomfort, balanced, we hope, by some Indian summer days.

We left the schoolhouse early yesterday and took some fast new expressways to Duluth where we lunched, elegantly and cheerfully, in the Hotel Duluth's Black Bear Room (a wandering bear barged into the bar one icy winter's day and lost his life thereby. Stuffed, he now dominates the bar.)

*(which became Knitter's Almanac).

Elizabeth Zimmermann

By evening we had snaked our way NE along the shore of Lake Superior to Grand Marais where there is a wonderfully friendly hotel which not only tolerates, but welcomes cats. crfl (sic) had been lodged at the cat-motel at home, but we had acceded to KLINE's pleading and brought him with us. He is behaving extremely well.

This morning we woke him early (or he us?), ploughed on Northwards, entered Canada at Pigeon River, bought our accustomed annual groceries and fishing license at Kakabeka Falls, and our liquids (gas, beer and firewater) at Ignace, turned sharp North again along 35 miles of very mixed dirt road to the Inputting Place.

For two days it had consistently fogged, misted, drizzled and downright rained, but as we crossed the bridge marked "Unsafe. Do not use", we realized things were drying up.

Having made a beautiful diagram of the boat with the proper places for all our duffel and gear, we followed it, and in 25 minutes everything was stowed away, the car parked and we took to the water - the English River. The sun promptly showed signs of coming out, the wind was a following one, the Old Man started the faithful motor and in just over an hour we were here, to find our island sparkling in the sunshine.

Now the tent is up, the cat KLINE is within it, resting from his excitement (he promenaded about the canoe on the way here, sniffing the air like an old sea-cat) and we are out after the first fish. That

means the Old Man is. I am supplied with light blue pen, my knitting, and the red Hudson Bay blanket. The third of these now looks very tempting and I shall try for a nap, walleyes and northerns permitting.

Tuesday Sept 28. It still writes. That was such a sound nap that I woke only on the catching of the 2nd walleye. We returned to camp, made a fire with the two-year-old wood, cooked coffee and walleye filets, admired the moon and two large stars, and crawled into the sack. In the night there were several heavy rain showers, but that was OK as everything was in the tent, including a loud-purring KLINE.

By morning there was only an early mist which dissipated and gave way to sunshine long enough for us to establish ourselves properly, cook a good breakfast of bacon and eggs and take off for Turner Island on our traditional visit.

Now it is raining in earnest; the Old Man paddles, trailing a fishline and I'm holed up under the boat-tarpaulin which I laboriously constructed out of heavy canvas for just such occasions as this.

Wed Sept 29. Quite literally no more time to write yesterday. Rain started and by 2 pm had increased to a downpour. So we resourcefully went to bed for 18 hours! While it was still light we made lightening sorties for food and drink, but the cat KLINE chose this time to suffer from a frightful cold in his furry chest and one of us felt it necessary to hold him snugly at all times so that he would not wander

dolefully about, shivering. He is, after all, an elderly kitten (11 years old) and a sedentary, indoor type at best.

The night, therefore, was a wild one. Rain pattered down deafeningly on the tent and the wind wailed and lashed through the tree-tops, but today has turned out perfectly.

Thurs. Sept 30. It may be hard to credit that late-September camping offers next to no time for entries in an almanac. The days are short to begin with, and then there is a promise given to the kids - promise _never_ to let Pop out alone in the boat: all right, I promise. Ever since he nearly drowned himself with the boat, miles from camp and me, this has been a family apprehension. At least if I am with him we can drown as a team.

Today I have broken the promise. It is raw and breezy and sunless. KLINE and I toast ourselves in the lee of some cedars by a radiant campfire and the Old Man is in the next bay, catching a giant Northern which instinct and experience tell him lurks in those waters. He has promised not to drown and I suppose I must be content with this. All the forenoon KLINE and I shared the boat with him, shivering and not complaining, but he felt the shivering I'm sure and has insisted on having us in the comfort of camp. Comfort is the word: the tent has been re-put up, I cook at waist-height on a large rock, a windbreak has been set up near the cookfire and bushes have been hacked back to give us a free waterfront runway to lookout-point to the West and a very small sandy beach

continued on next page

to the East. This is where KLINE and I now sit, full of warmed-up kedgeree and coffee and well-content. For warming-up a campfire is just right; anything put near it or over it - kedgeree and coffee respectively - automatically warms in no time. For cooking I prefer a small powerful fire and my fireirons. I build the fire with birch bark (from dead birches, naturally) dry twigs (the lower ones from a fir tree burn best) and "made" firewood about 8 - 10" long, sawn and split by the Old Man. It is set between two level rocks about 12-15" apart, with usually an unlevel rock at the back. From level rock to level rock run my fireirons, of 2" iron about 18" long. These are enough to balance any pot and with skillful management of the fire can take two pots side-by-side. They travel and spend 50 weeks of the year in a long narrow canvas bag, sooty within and fairly clean without. The whole contraption is usually on the ground (crouch crouch) and happy is the camp with a rock of sufficient size and

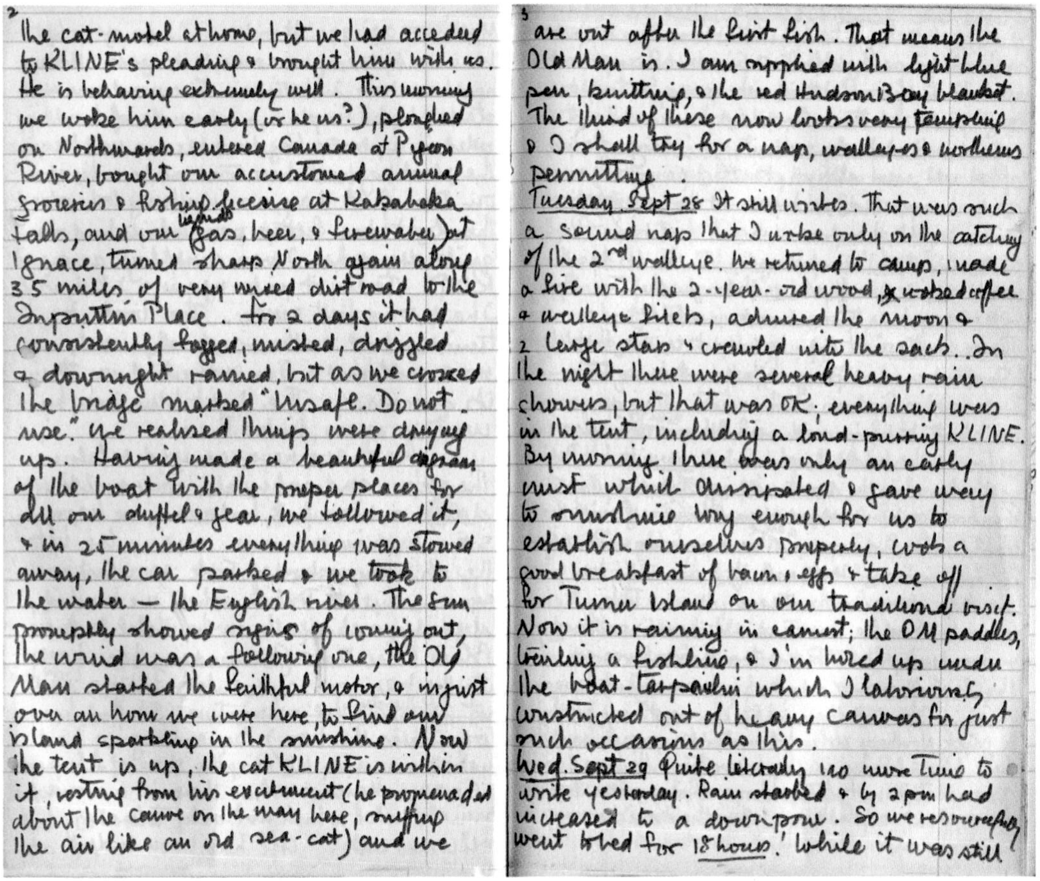

approximate height to contain my "work stove". This is such a camp and today's kedgeree was outstanding made by an upstanding cook.

Surprise. At that very instant came the familiar patter-patter. KLINE and I have abandoned the campfire to its spitting and hissing fate, along with a pot of coffee-

water, hopefully suspended over it, and have retired to the tent. He kneads himself a bed on my heavy camp sweater, which he prefers to all the Hudson's Bay blankets and down jackets offered to him. I don't blame him; it is made of beautiful old dark Oatmeal Sheepsdown with a natty

Tyrolese border of Loden green and black. Over the years it has lengthened to a 3/4 coat and it is the sweater which had it's pockets removed and re-inserted much higher up. A hole was burned in it once and was faultlessly repaired (in garter-st, mind you) in unmatching wool. It sports large beautiful pewter buttons, brought back by Lissa from Salzburg. The "wrong" side of the garter-stitch colour-stripes has been overcast - every stitch - in the appropriate colour so that it may be worn either way. It is a beloved garment and if I am ever buried, I hope it will be my shroud.

At that point the Old Man returned, fishless and shining with wet, but dry under his rain gear. On his

sound recommendation we pepped up the campfire and stretched a large piece of plastic tarp behind it, under which we now sit, dry, warm and moderately philosophical. The fire is strong enough to defy the rain, which drips companionably on our feet.

Handwritten journal pages (center):

the cat-model at home, but we had acceded to KLINE's pleading & brought him with us. He is behaving extremely well. This morning we woke him early (or he us?), ploughed on Northwards, entered Canada at Pigeon River, bought our accustomed animal groceries & fishing license at Kakabeka Falls, and our gas, beer, & firewater at Ignace, turned sharp North again along 35 miles of very mixed dirt road to the Inportun Place. For 2 days it had consistently fogged, misted, drizzled & downright rained, but as we crossed the bridge marked "Unsafe. Do not use." we realised things were drying up. Having made a beautiful diagram of the boat with the proper places for all our duffel & gear, we followed it, & in 25 minutes everything was stowed away, the car parked & we took to the water — the English river. The sun promptly showed signs of coming out, the wind was a following one, the Old Man started the faithful motor, & in just over an hour we were here, to find our island sparkling in the sunshine. Now the tent is up, the cat KLINE is within it, resting from his excitement (he promenaded about the canoe on the way here, sniffing the air like an old sea-cat) and we

are out after the first fish. That means the Old Man is. I am supplied with light-blue pen, knitting, & the red Hudson Bay blanket. The third of these now looks very tempting & I shall try for a nap, walleyes & northerns permitting.

Tuesday Sept 28 It still writes. That was such a sound nap that I woke only on the catching of the 2nd walleye. We returned to camp, made a fire with the 2-year-old wood, & cooked coffee & walleye fillets, admired the moon & 2 large stars & crawled into the sack. In the night there were several heavy rain showers, but that was OK: everything was in the tent, including a loud-purring KLINE. By morning there was only an early crust which dissipated & gave way to sunshine long enough for us to establish ourselves properly, cook a good breakfast of bacon, eggs & take off for Tumar Island on our traditional visit. Now it is raining in earnest; the O.M. paddles, trailing a fishline, & I'm holed up under the boat-tarpaulin which I laboriously constructed out of heavy canvas for just such occasions as this.

Wed. Sept 29 Quite literally no more time to write yesterday. Rain started & by 2pm had increased to a downpour. So we resourcefully went to bed for 18 hours! While it was still

I cannot speak too highly in praise of my boots. They are the foot-part of a pair of cheap and nasty waders, which leaked long before their time. We amputated the feet which turned out to be a _most_ serviceable pair of short rubber boots and I'll never come camping without them again, as they have changed my camp-life. They can be stepped into or chucked off without all that elaborate lacing up necessary with the professional-looking hunting boots. Having cleated soles, they slip only on the slickest of rocks. They carry you dry through water up to 12" deep and enable you to wash face, clean teeth or rinse dishes standing comfortably _in_ the water instead of teetering on the brink in imminent peril of a smart dive. When they wear out I am spiritually prepared to buy as replacement a pair of L.L. Bean's short boots, which I now admit to being worth every penny of $11.95 and more.

Here we sit then, both of us warmed by the fire and the coffee we made over it, content with ourselves and our resourcefulness and both scribbling away like mad. Rolled up in our bedroll since last year, we found fragments of a camping diary sporadically kept by the Old Man for several years, including the time we spent at this very campsite. Read it aloud, I said. He grimaced and started reading as from a very drivelling book, accenting all words equally. Very soon however, he became caught up in his own words and doings, was carried away, and read like a human being. Inspired, he is now adding to this chronicle.

As for me, my pen pales; I fear she runs dry; I shall cap her for today.

Fri Oct 1st (blank)

Sat Oct 2. A typical Oct day in the real, not the sentimental sense of the word. An East wind, grey skies and sporadic rain drops on the tent. I take a moment to write while the Old Man snatches brief period between showers to wash and clean teeth. I find more and more that a writer in this family garners little time and no sympathy for the practice of the craft. But the little blue pen still writes, which is cheering. That was a quick wash; here he is again.

Yesterday I kept myself busy and happy de-pilling the heavy camp sweater and thinking about pilling in general, which is rather over-feared. Individual wool fibers like to stick to each other and with a little friction, tend to roll themselves up into small balls. This is what happened to the wool fibers that stick up from the surface of a sweater, or carpet, or blanket. Once they - in the form of small balls - have been removed, there are no fibers left sticking up from the surface, so there are no more pills. Some very tightly-twisted wools seem to make no pills at all.

But if you have a garment that has pilled, set aside an hour for dealing with it and pick off the pills methodically, section by section: sleeve, front, sleeve, other front, back. Thus the undone bits can be compared to the done bits for thoroughness of de-pilling. Hold the surface up to the light from time to time, to spot pills which have escaped you. When the job is done, it is rarely necessary to repeat it on a given garment.

The Modular Tomten (next page), knitted by Elizabeth

Elizabeth Zimmermann

E L I Z A B E T H   Z I M M E R M A N N
BOX 5555   MILWAUKEE 11, WIS.

Newsletter and Leaflet #7.   Fall 1961.
Free to all current customers. Extra copies 25¢.

Dear Knitter,
      Someone told me that this fall's Tyrolese garter-stitch jacket has the modular quality of architecture, so I looked up "modular", & quite agree; the number of stitches around the thing are divided by 4 and 8 to determine the shape, & they keep recurring.

DIRECTIONS

BODY - (For pockets, see below) Cast on 112 sts. for total width of sweater. Work 10 ridges. (1 ridge = 2 rows.) To give a good shape to the back, work a "short ridge", i.e. K 84, turn, K 56, turn K to end of row. Rep. this every 10 ridges.

ARMHOLES - At 40 ridges, K 14 for R front,
                      cast off 28 for R armhole,
                      K 28 for back,
                      cast off 28 for L armhole,
                      K 14 for L front.

Work each section separately for 28 ridges. Do not cast off.

COLLAR - Put all 56 sts. of fronts & back on one needle & work for 7 ridges. Cast off.

SLEEVES - From right side, pick up 56 sts. from the ridges of the sides of armholes. Work 14 ridges. Mark 3 centre sts. Decr. 1 st. each side of these every 3rd ridge until 28 sts. remain, or to desired length for sleeve. Cast off. Sew rest of armholes & sleeves.

That's it. Notice the multiples? 112, 56, 28, 14, 7 ?
Now here are some variations & embellishments:-

HOOD - Start off as for collar with 56 sts, & inc. 2 sts. at centre every 2nd row 7 times. (70 sts.) Work 28 ridges. K to centre of row, & weave halves together to form hood.

TO WEAVE GARTER ST - Holding needles parallel, thread yarn through blunt needle. * Pass yarn through 1st st. on front needle as if to K, sl. st. off. Pass yarn through 2nd st. on front needle as if to P, leave st. on. Rep from * on back needle. Rep from * on front & back needles alternately until all sts. are used up. Adjust weaving thread for correct tension.

Ten years after this Newsletter was published, Elizabeth added the design to *Knitting Without Tears* and changed its name to Modular Tomten Jacket; it is proving to be a timeless design.

She first knitted this little, hooded jacket around 1940, for her infant son. It was inherited, in turn, by his two sisters and remains a cherished object to this day.

The variations are numerous:
- hood, collar or cardigan neck
- buttons, clasps or zipper
- solid, stripes or slip-stitch pattern
- texture patterns or handpainted wool

Note: I no longer cast off the underarm stitches, but put them on a piece of wool. Then, after you have picked up stitches around the armhole and begin to work the sleeve back-and-forth: at the end of each row knit the last sleeve stitch together with a stitch from the holder until they have all been absorbed. Continue the sleeve as instructed.

E l i z a b e t h   Z i m m e r m a n n

POCKETS - First make 2 pieces 14 sts. wide & 10 ridges long. After
14 ridges of body, K 7, * put next 14 sts. on thread, K 1 piece
on to R needle, K to within 21 sts. of end of row, rep. from *.
When jacket is done, cast off sts. on thread (with another colour if
you like). Sew linings in place from the wrong side.
BORDERS - With right side toward you, & starting at R lower edge,
pick up 1 st. for each ridge around front, including neck or
collar. Work 1 or 2 ridges in contrasting colour(s). Cast off on
wrong side, working neck-back very tightly. A 4-ridge border of
2-ply Loden yarn doubled looks good on the pockets, tops of sleeves,
cuffs, & front edges of a Sheepsdown sweater. Make mitred corners
at neck fronts by increasing 2 sts. at these points every 2nd row.
CARDIGAN NECKLINE - After 61 ridges of fronts have been completed,→
cast off 7 sts. at outer edge. Cast off 1 more st. every 2nd row
until all sts. are used up. Sts. may be left on thread & included in border.

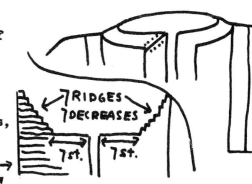

You can make 4 sizes from these directions by changing weight of yarn & needle-size (& thus GAUGE).
By varying the cast-on sts. in multiples of 8, you can make any size you want in any yarn you please.

SIZE	WIDTH	MATERIAL	GAUGE	NEEDLE SIZE I USE
Baby	22"	3 skeins Fisherman Yarn	5 st. to 1"	#4 (You may needle larger or smaller
Child	27"	4 skeins 3-ply Sheepswool	4 st. to 1"	#6 needles, depending upon how tightly
Child	32"	5 skeins 4-ply Sheepswool	3½ st. to 1"	#8 or how loosely you knit.)
Adult	40"	8 skeins Sheepsdown	3 st. to 1"	#10½

These measurements are of the sweater itself; the recipient should be slightly less around, especially
the adult. Sheepsdown is so thick that it should be made extra large to leave room for the wearer.

Make these jackets in Oatmeal, Cream, Grey, or Black, with Red-&-Green or Black-&-Green trim. Silver or
staghorn buttons. Zippers for children. Try a belt in the back, or scarlet pocket-linings. When you
pick up sts. or change colours, & the back shows, overcast the showing sts. with yarn at ½-thickness, 3 or
4 times in each stitch. Knit a soft white lining for a baby's hood, & thread a tie between this & the
hood, to tie beneath chin. Thread another string around cuffs, & tie tightly. Now you have coat, cap,
& mittens in one. Next year, take strings out. Year after, put them in again, ready for next baby.
The original lasted for 3 babies. If you want to make a matching pram-cover, ask me; no more room for
that here. Have you noticed that I leave sts on a thread, not a holder? Much more practical.
In garter-st I cast off on the wrong side. I slip all 1st sts; it's years since I knitted a 1st st.
Sad news; "Guernsey & Jersey Patterns" is out of print. Cherish
yours, & lend sparingly. Boastful news; my revolutionary
Sideways Sock has been bought by Woman's Day. Watch for it.
STOP PRESS. Enclosed reprint from the Milwaukee Journal shows the
above sweater in a large man's size (128 st). 9 skeins Sheepsdown.
The other model was in McCall's; directions & graph, 25¢.

Sincerely
Elizabeth

By eliminating the cast-off-underarm ridge, you can provide
greater elasticity for the armhole and save yourself having to
sew a seam.

I also like to knit EZ's Applied I-Cord border up the
front, around the hood (or collar) and down the other side -
into which you can incorporate Looped or Hidden I-Cord
buttonholes. You can continue to motor around lower edge as
well and border the entire periphery with I-Cord.

A knitter writes, "It isn't surprising to see Elizabeth
Zimmermann's patterns mentioned as Popular Repeat Items.
My favorite is the Tomten, of which I have made seven.
Maybe because she gives such latitude in following her
patterns, it's hard to get bored."

knitted by Meg Swansen

Elizabeth Zimmermann

knitted by Meg Swansen

both knitted by Alison Albrecht

knitted by Elaine Wedeking

knitted by Alison Albrecht

knitted by Elizabeth Zimmermann

Elizabeth Zimmermann

knitted by Meg Swansen

The Opinionated Knitter

Elizabeth Zimmermann

ELIZABETH ZIMMERMANN
BOX 5555   MILWAUKEE 11, WIS.

Dear Knitter,

The Wisconsin winter has been long & stubborn, but soon now we shall be listening for the geese. My husband is down at the river, ice-fishing, muffled to the gills in his watchcap and his old honourable sweater, his toes happy in Sheepswool socks. I hug the logging-stove, & work on this, the spring newsletter.

Directions are for the classic raglan sweater, made from the bottom up on circular needles. Body & sleeves are worked separately to the armholes; then all but the underarm sts. are put on one needle, & decreased up to the neck in raglan shaping. Underarms are woven later. The number of sts. cast on depends on your personal measurements & the GAUGE of your knitting. GAUGE means the number of sts. to one inch. To determine GAUGE, make a swatch of 24 sts. with the yarn and needle you plan to use. Be sure to count the number of sts. to 3 inches, & divide by 3, to ensure taking an average inch as a sample. Multiply the result by the inches around, & you will have the number of sts. you need. Below are directions for a sweater 40" around at a GAUGE of 5 sts. to 1". I used a #5 needle, but you may knit tighter or looser than I do, & thus need a larger or smaller size. Figures in parentheses will serve as a percentage guide if your sweater has more or less sts. than mine does.

CIRCULAR SEAMLESS RAGLAN SWEATER. 40" around, 23" long. GAUGE 5 st. to 1"
MATERIALS. 3 skeins "Homespun", or 4 skeins 2-ply Sheepswool, or
    5 skeins Fisherman Yarn. One 24" & one 16" circular needle of a size to give a GAUGE of 5 st. to 1".
BODY. With 24" needle, cast on 200 sts. Join, being careful not to
    twist, & Knit for 14½". Put 16 sts. (8% of 200 sts of body) on thread at each underarm. Set aside, & start....
SLEEVE. With 16" needle, cast on 40 sts. (20% of 200). It may be hard
    to knit around for the first few rnds; if so, use 4 needles. Increase 2 sts. at underarm avery 5 rnds, & you will soon be able to use the circular needle. When you have 66 sts. (33% of 200), work straight until sleeve measures 18". Put 16 sts. at underarm on thread. Work another sleeve. Put all sts. of body & sleeves on 24" needle, matching underarms (see diagram), & work straight for 1".
RAGLAN SHOULDERS. Mark 4 raglan points (X) at the spots where sleeves
    join body, with 84 sts. on front, 84 sts. on back, & 50 sts. on each sleeve. Decrease 2 sts. (sl 1, K 2 tog, psso) at markers every 2nd rnd, keeping the decreases in line. Continue decreasing steadily until 10 sts. (5% of 200) remain at top of each sleeve.
NECK SHAPING. At Left front raglan-marker K 5, cast off 34. Now
    work back & forth on circular needle, continuing to decrease every 2nd row at raglan points until remaining front & sleeve sts. have been miraculously used up. If you want a cardigan, now is the time to cut down front, (see below). For a slipover, pick up about 46 sts. on front & sides of neck, decrease 10% (K 8, K 2 tog around), & finish with 1 inch of ribbing or garter-st. Weave underarms.
BORDERS. Pick up all sts. of cuffs and/or lower edge. Decrease 10%
    & work 1 inch to correspond with neck. Block.

FOR 3/4 SLEEVES. Cast on 50 sts. (25% of 200). Inc 2 sts. every 5th rnd. to 66 sts. Work until 12" long.
RAGLAN VARIATIONS. You may decrease any way you wish as long as you eliminate 8 sts. every 2nd rnd. Try
    K 2 tog, P 1, sl 1, K 1, psso (pass sl st over). Or decr. 1 st. each side of 4 cables at raglan points.
FOR YOKE EFFECT. An inch or so after beginning raglan shaping, introduce a small pattern in another
    colour. Or make a solid colour yoke. Or a striped one. Or several pattenns. What you will.
FOR A CARDIGAN. Baste down centre front. With small st. & loose tension, sew on machine twice each side
    of basting. Cut on basting. Pick up 2 sts. for every 3 rows up Right edge, then around neck, & down Left edge. Mitre neck-front by increasing 2 sts. at this point every 2nd row. Make 6 or 7 3-stitch buttonholes on Right side. After 11 rows, cast off. Neaten cut edges with herringbone stitch.

AFTERTHOUGHT POCKETS. Try on sweater, & mark the place where you would like pockets. Snip 1 st. at centre
   of this, & unravel 10 sts. in each direction. Pick up resulting 40 sts. on 4 needles & work around
for 20 rnds. Fold pocket flat & sew or weave tog. You may put these pockets in boughten sweaters too.

All the "Homespun" colours are now available on special order in 2-ply, v. beautiful. Same price,
1.80 per generous 3 oz. skein. Six to seven skeins make an average sweater.

Gladys Thompson Round-up. If any one of the hundreds who bought "Guernsey and Jersey Patterns" (now,
alas, quite out of print) is not using this book, would she like to return it to me for the full $4
refund? It will bring cheer to someone on a long, pitiful, and almost hopeless waiting-list.

As I do not advertise, you customers are to be thanked for the gratifying briskness of my business.
I want to give my thanks tangible form, so if you recommend my yarns to a new customer, ask her to men-
-tion your name when she sends in her first order, & I will send you a present of your choice of a circu-
-lar needle; sizes 2 through 8, also 10½, in 24" & 16" lengths. This goes into effect in March 1962.

Two of my Sheepsdown caps are to appear in Woman's Day; next winter, I imagine. They are a Swirled Hat
& a Garter-stitch Pillbox. See if you can spot them.

Last summer's camping trip included portaging, so gear was reduced to a minimum. I took only six skeins
of "Homespun", & achieved six pairs of ribbed socks (60 sts on #3 needles) which are so far wearing very
well. They were rewarding to work on, could be slipped into a pocket, & were snatched up to be worn as
soon as completed. Canadian yarn, Canadian waters, & some ends left behind for Canadian mousenests.

The Opinionated Knitter

knitted by Maxene Mollen

Elizabeth Zimmermann

knitted by Meg Swansen

The Opinionated Knitter

Elizabeth Zimmermann

ELIZABETH ZIMMERMANN
BOX 5555   MILWAUKEE 11, WIS.

Newsletter and leaflet # 9   Fall 1962.
Free until Spring '63; than 25¢.   Extra copies 25¢.

Dear Knitter,
     My available leaflets now cover important basic sweaters, as follows:-

1. Shetland sweater with Fair Isle yoke.
2. Scandinavian drop-shouldered ski-sweaters.
4. Seamless classic Brooks sweater or cardigan.
5. Sheepsdown sweater & Watchcap in Prime Rib.

6. Circular Aran sweater or cardigan.
7. Bavarian jackets, in garter-stitch.
8. Seamless raglan sweater or cardigan.
(All models but 5 & 7 are for circular needle.)

Tell me what other designs you want; I will be guided by your comments in future newsletters.

Now I have a knitted blanket for you. Afghans welter in a multi-coloured doldrums, and I would suggest that you try variety in texture for a change. Directions below are for a fine thick, light blanket, with a great quality of cosiness, its neutral shade fitting well into any room. It is made in plain garter-stitch (beginners' heaven), of only four pieces, and I did it on a 4-day car trip. Interest lies in corners turned in the knitted fabric, and in the resulting variations of light and shade. The design is based on a square 24 sts wide and 24 ridges (48 rows) long. By varying the number of stitches and ridges, larger or smaller sizes may be made.

KNITTED GARTER STITCH BLANKET IN SHEEPSDOWN.
GAUGE. Approximately 2 sts. to 1".
MATERIALS. 10 skeins Sheepsdown, 1 pr #15 needles.
SIZE WHEN COMPLETED. Approximately 42" X 68".
STITCH PATTERN. K all stitches. Slip 1st stitch, and P last stitch for braid-like edge.

PIECE A. (make 2) Cast on 24 sts. Work 24 ridges, (48 rows). Now turn a corner, by knitting 1 st. less every 2nd row, as follows:-
Work to within 1 st. of end of row, turn, work back.
"   "   2 sts.   "   "   "   "
"   "   3 sts.   "   "   "   "
Continue in this way, leaving all unknitted sts. diagonally on needle, until 2 sts. remain. You are now at outer point of corner ✗. Complete corner by knitting 1 st. more every 2nd row, as follows:-
Work 3 sts, turn, work back.
"   4 sts,   "   "
"   5 sts,   "   "

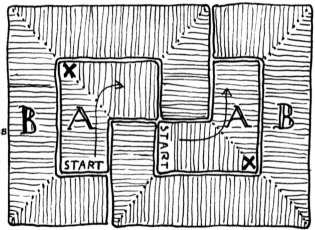

There are several satisfying features to this design:

The wool is her lovely, soft, thick *Sheepsdown*, so the work goes very quickly. (Because I can knit a 4-ounce skein in under an hour, I don't even bother winding it into a ball -- but knit directly from my swift.)

You can vary the design by changing colors for each of the four segments - or even for each of the 12 areas between corner-turns.

This afghan is totally reversible - one of the many endearing aspects of garter-stitch.

Note: take a stronger (spun and plied) wool for sewing the sections together.

Baby blanket in 3-ply Sheepswool. Cast on 72 sts and simply make 4 corners. Weave beginning and end together.

Continue in this way until all sts. have been knitted again. <u>Corner completed</u>; and you still have your 24 sts. Work 24 ridges. Cast off.
<u>PIECE B</u>. (make 2) Cast on 24 sts. Work 24 ridges, turn corner (as above), work 48 ridges, turn corner in same direction, work 48 ridges, turn corner in same direction again, work 24 ridges. Cast off. Assemble the four pieces neatly with finer yarn, by weaving sts. from each side alternately.

The above directions will give you:-
In 4-ply Sheepswool (3 sts. to 1") a 32" X 48" blanket. (8 skeins)
In 3-ply Sheepswool (4 sts. to 1") a 24" X 36" blanket. (4 skeins)
In 2-ply Sheepswool (5 sts. to 1") a 20" X 30" pram-cover. (2 skeins)

<u>Approximate</u> needle sizes.
10½
8
5

In McCall's Needlework Fall-Winter '62-'63 the middle sweater on p.42 is mine. 6 - 8 skeins Sheepsdown in Cream, 1 in Oatmeal, 1 skein ea. White and Black Fisherman Yarn (doubled). I prefer this sweater held in at the lower edge by pyjama elastic through the hem, but my spies tell me that fashionable skiers like them bell-shaped... My woolly hats are still pending in Woman's Day, and they are also bringing one of my Arans; #6 with a slight improvement. Can you spot it?

If you don't need your "Guernsey and Jersey Patterns", I can still offer the full $4 refund.

That indispensible primer and manual "The Mary Thomas Knitting Book" is out of print, but I have managed to obtain a modest stack from England. $3.50, including postage.

Also I have a few "Tricots Enfants" put out by "Jardin des Modes" in Paris. These charmingly simple childrens' designs (31 of them) are of course explained in undiluted French, but are supplied with exact diagrams and life-sized photographs of stitches used. $1 including postage.

You receive a bonus circular needle for each new customer you recommend if with her <u>first order</u> She gives your name and needle-size and -length you wish. (sizes 2-8, also 10½, 16" or 24" long.)

For rush orders, include 35¢ for SPECIAL HANDLING, and packet goes PO to PO as fast as a letter.

To blend almost-matching yarns, work alternate rows of them for an inch or so.

I don't like zippers in sweaters, but many recipients insist, so I give in. I find that washing (or blocking) garment and zipper separately before assembling helps with stretching and shrinking problems. I sew them in neatly, by hand, on the right side, muttering to myself.

Sincerely
Elizabeth

A number of years ago, the mill that custom spun this wool for us reduced the length-per-skein by 30 yards, but kept the weight at 4oz; how DID they do that and still maintain the same strand-diameter?

So, no longer can you knit one of these afghans from only 10 skeins; it is more like 14-16 skeins at present.

See other Sheepsdown designs on pages 30 and 94 and add skeins to the recommended number.

Sheepsdown Afghan (NL #9) knitted by Meg Swansen
Pillbox Hat (NL #11, page 60) knitted by Jane Lippmann
Baby Surprise Jacket (NL#21, page 102) knitted by Lloie Schwartz
Leggings (NL#17, page 88) knitted by Elizabeth Zimmermann
Bootees (NL#22, page 108) knitted by Greg Cotton

If you wish to eliminate the large holes along the diagonal, you may employ "wrapping" as follows:

- knit to the turning point
- slip next stitch to R needle
- bring wool to the front (between the needles)
- return slipped stitch to L needle
- turn and work back.

Since this is garter-stitch, you may either knit the wrap and the slipped stitch together – or ignore the wrap and simply knit the slipped stitch as, left in place, the wrap resembles a purl-bump and harmonizes with the rest of the fabric. Experiment and see which you like best.

Elizabeth Zimmermann

I bordered this afghan in a contrasting shade, using EZ's Applied I-Cord trim with Joyce Williams' Variation as follows:

With a smaller size needle, a few inches from one corner, pick up one stitch for each ridge along the selvedge. It doesn't matter which strand you choose, just remain consistent.

On Afghan-sized needle, Cast On 2 (or 3) stitches (depending upon how large you want the I-Cord tube to be). Immediately transfer them to the pick-up needle and *k 1 (or 2), slip 1, yo, knit 1 (picked-up stitch), p2sso (being the slipped stitch plus the yo). Replace the 2 (or 3) stitches to the L needle and repeat from *.

When you come to the corner stitch, work all 3 Cord stitches without attaching them to the blanket; attach the corner stitch; work another unattached Cord round. Proceed. Those two unattached rounds will provide an extra bit of fabric to help the Cord swing around the corner.

The yarn-over covers contrasting-color blips which may peek-through, and is a refinement of Joyce Williams'.

Elizabeth Zimmermann

ELIZABETH ZIMMERMANN
BOX 5555   MILWAUKEE 11, WISCONSIN

Dear Knitter,
              Directions for socks, timeless
boosters of the male ego, are what many of you
seem to want. If you own a "Mary Thomas Knitting
Book",(3.50, postpaid) you will find 22 of the 245
pages devoted to this far-reaching subject. Here
is the way I make them. (Reprinted from Woman's
Day Magazine, a Fawcett publication.)
For very enduring High School socks, use Fisherman
Yarn at a gauge of 5 sts to 1", and the same
directions. White Fisherman washes excellently.
For men who like wool socks for the office, try
"Homespun" with 60 sts, and a gauge of 6 sts to 1"
In all cases I incorporate nylon thread in heels
and toes.
Use up odd yarns for tops and toes.
One of my dear cussies takes 4-ply Sheepswool to
make Deep-sea Divers' stockings.
2-ply Sheepswool is not really good for socks.

Now I carry the "Mary Thomas Book of Knitting
Patterns", 3.50, postpaid. It contains hundreds
of patterns, and many unexpected usefulnesses,
such as translations of French and German
knitting terms.

Instructions for
these socks are also
published in
Elizabeth's fourth
book, *Knitting
Around* and include
some color-pattern
possibilities.

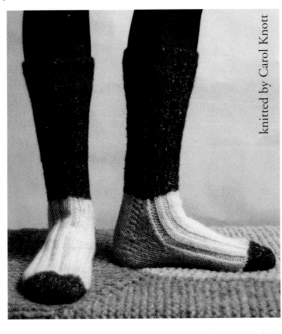

knitted by Carol Knott

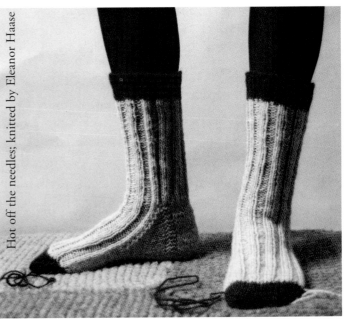

Hot off the needles; knitted by Eleanor Haase

Sold my "Hawser" sweater to McCall's Needlework
for next winter. You can't miss it, with its
three large knitted-in rope patterns around the
yoke. Subtle back-of-neck shaping, too.

My thanks to all who so charmingly recommend my
yarns. Be sure to ask the recommendee to tell
me, with her first order, the size and length of
the free circular needle you would like.
Sizes 2-8, also 10½, in 16" and 24" lengths.

Many of you ask how I wash my sweaters. I use
lukewarm water, any good mild detergent I have
around -- Lux, Fab, Woolite -- and I work fast,
expelling as much rinsewater as possible in the
spinner of my Easy. Or you can go into the
garden and swing your sweater round your head in
a salad-basket, or roll it in a towel and jump on
it, like Mr Gladstone. Then dry flat, moulding
into shape; a damp sweater is almost like clay in
this respect. If you have a ribbed edge, turn
it up, like this ———>
But NEVER let a sweater
lie in a wet heap.

We made a lovely coat of handwoven cream-coloured
Irish tweed from Carol Brown. Knitted sleeves of
Sheepswool, and a raw silk lining. Write to
Carol for samples at Putney, Vermont.

A small plea; I do appreciate payment with order.
This eases my bookkeeping, saving time for me, and
thus money for you in the long run. If uncertain
of amount, some even send blank cheques, as I am
perfectly honest. But no C.O.D.s -- I would
sooner bill you.

Now, have a good summer. Dabble your feet in the
water, and fill the sock-drawer against next
winter. I find this as satisfying as studying
seed-catalogues by a roaring January fire, or,
this year, a roaring March fire...

Sincerely, Elizabeth.

Woodsman's Socks

SIZES: 10–12 (see Sock Size Chart under General Directions).

MATERIALS: 3-ply natural sheep's wool (to order see information under ski mittens, page 107), or 4-ply sports yarn used double throughout, 5 oz. color A, 1 oz. color B; dp knitting needles, 1 set (4) No. 6 (English needles No. 7).

GAUGE: (Stockinette st) 4 sts = 1"; 6 rows = 1".

Starting at cuff with B, cast on 44 sts. Divide sts with 22 sts on first needle and 11 sts each on 2nd and 3rd needles. Work in ribbing of p 2, k 2 for 1½". Break off B. Attach A, and continue in ribbing until piece measures 8" from beg.

Heel Flap: Work on first needle only. **1st row**: Sl 1, k 20, p 1. **2nd row**: Sl 1, k 3, p 14, k 3, p 1. Repeat first and 2nd rows until flap measures 3", ending on wrong side.

To Turn Heel: **1st row**: Sl 1, k 10, sl 1, k 1, psso, k 1, turn. **2nd row**: Sl 1, p 2, p 2 tog, p 1, turn. **3rd row**: Sl 1, k 3, sl 1, psso, k 1, turn. **4th row**: Sl 1, p 4, p 2 tog, p 1, turn. **5th row**: Sl 1, k 5, sl 1, k 1, psso, k 1, turn. **6th row**: Sl 1, p 6, p 2 tog, p 1, turn. **7th row**: Sl 1, k 7, sl 1, k 1, psso, k 1, turn. **8th row**: Sl 1, p 8, p 2 tog, p 1, turn. **9th row**: Sl 1, k 9, sl 1, k 1, psso, k 1, turn. **10th row**: Sl 1, p 10, p 2 tog (12 sts).

To Shape Gussets: **1st rnd**: 1st needle (heel needle): Sl 1, k 11, pick up and k 13 sts along side of heel flap. 2nd needle: Rib across 2nd and 3rd needles (instep needle). 3rd needle: Pick up and k 13 sts along side of heel flap and 6 sts from first needle (60 sts). **2nd rnd**: 1st needle: K to within last 2 sts, k 2 tog. 2nd needle: Work in ribbing. 3rd needle: Sl 1, k 1, psso, k across. **3rd rnd**: K across first and 3rd needles, and rib across 2nd needle. Repeat 2nd and 3rd rnds 7 times more (44 sts). Work even, keeping 2nd needle in ribbing, until sock is 2½" less than desired length (see Sock Size Chart). Break off A, attach B.

To Shape Toe: **1st row**: 1st needle: K to within last 4 sts, k 2 tog, k 2. 2nd needle: K 2, sl 1, k 1, psso, k to within last 4 sts, k 2 tog, k 2. 3rd needle: K 2, sl 1, k 1, psso, k to end. **2nd row**: K around. Repeat first and 2nd rows until 20 sts remain. Break off. Weave toe tog using Kitchener Stitch

Elizabeth Zimmermann

ELIZABETH ZIMMERMANN
BOX 5555   MILWAUKEE 11, WIS. 53211

Newsletter and leaflet #11   Fall 1963
free until Spring '64; then 25¢. Extra copies 25¢.

Dear Knitter,
   Consider the advantages of knitted headgear. Knitted caps are fast and easy to make.
(at least, I think mine are) They draw praise and admiration, and use up odds and ends of yarn. They
are warm and comfortable to wear, and easy to wash. This adds up to pleasant knitting for presents,
and excellent profit-making for bazaars. People will fairly easily pay $5 for something snappy to put
on their heads, though they boggle at $1.95 for mittens. (And mittens are more work, and dull to make.)

Here are some good caps, all in Fisherman Yarn or 2-ply Sheepswool, on a 16" circular needle, at a
GAUGE of 5 sts to 1". I take a #5 needle. You may need a different size, depending on your knitting
tension. Each cap uses under 1 skein. Put in colour patterns if and as you wish. (see leaflet #2, 25¢)
They can be worked in yarn oddments, doubled, if thin, or even thribbled, since patterns may well be
slightly heavier than background. For caps with heavier yarn at 4 sts. to 1", cast on 20% less stitches.

PILLBOX Cast on 91 sts. Join. K around for $\frac{1}{2}$" for hem. P 1 rnd. K straight
for 3$\frac{1}{2}$". P 1 rnd. Shape for top:- Decr. 7 sts. evenly spaced around. (i.e. K 11,
K 2 tog. around.) K 1 rnd. Rep. these 2 rnds. until there are 49 sts. Change to
4 needles, and decr. every rnd. until there are 7 sts. Finish off. Sew up hem
with many loose stitches. Dampen, and block over canister 6" in diameter.

SKI-BONNET Totally adjustable; fits all ages. Cast on 77 sts. Join. K 4".
Shape top as for pillbox. To form back of neck, baste a straight line from edge
to beg of decr. Machine-stitch twice on each side of basting. Cut on basting.
With right side towards you, pick up 18 sts. along R cut edge, 74 sts. along front
edge, 18 sts. along L cut edge, and 2 sts. at centre back. K around for 1".
P 1 rnd. K 1". Do not cast off, but pull needle out and sew sts. down on wrong
side, forming hem. Make a 2 yd cord and thread through hem, knotting at back
of neck. Pull out loops at corners for ties.

HEADBAND Cast on 90 sts. Join. P 1 rnd. K $\frac{1}{2}$". Shape for back:- K 15, turn.
P 30, turn. K 35, turn. P 40, turn. K 45, turn. P 50, turn. K 55, turn.
P 60, turn. K for 1$\frac{1}{2}$". P 1 rnd. Change colour and work lining to correspond.
Do not cast off, but pull needle out, and weave end cunningly to beginning.
You can embellish lining with fitting thoughts: "Ski-Heil", "Vorlage ","Meister-
-wedler". Work out alphabet 5 squares high on graph paper, and knit letters in.

V. WARM HAT Reversible, good for M or F, and wearable as many ways as there are
people. Cast on 91 sts. Join. P 1 rnd. K 6" (or more), and shape top as for
pillbox. For lining, with right side towards you, pick up 91 sts. around edge in
different colour, and repeat process. This is our favourite cap at the moment.

About buttonholes on both sides: people rarely concern
themselves with male/female sides for buttonholes anymore.

However, if you *do* care, Juliet Crisp taught us a way to
remember which side is which: "Women are always right."

And, if anyone still wishes for a FAST CAP, make a pillbox 5" deep without hem or
P rnd, but with a ribbed or garter-st edge. Leaving 18 sts. for back and 37 sts.
for front, pick up 18 sts. for each earflap. Work 1" on these 18 sts, and then
decr. 1 st. at beg of each row down to nothing. Make ties of Idiot's Delight,
(see Mary Thomas Knitting Book, p.124) and add long cord with bobble. Ski-tows
frown on long cords.

THOUGHTS AND COMMENT
Girls love to inherit boys' cardigans, but the reverse is not true. Make buttonholes on both sides.
Seeing to it that buttons are on R side before you even ask boy to try it on might help matters.

This leads me to BUTTONS. Yardland Farm Ltd of Route 2, East Troy, Wis. announces the first in its
series of Country Buttons in fine blending shades of synthetic turquoise, mounted in light weight
aluminum, 7/8" in diameter, at $1 each. They are perfect with Robin Egg Blue "Homespun", as an
accent with the other colours, or as an ornament for a man's sport jacket. Order from Yardland Farm.

I am gingerly walking around the edge of the button business myself. The flat round bone ones I
ordered are here from Germany,(3/4" across), and the spindle-shaped bone ones have arrived from
Mexico.(1¼" long). Either solves the problem of what to use with Cream Sheepswool. 25¢ each, from me.

Sorry I misled you about my "Hawser" sweater; it is not in this winter's McCall's Needlework. Perhaps
next year? Woman's Day has bought my new heavy Aran cardigan, a Loden and Cream 3-ply Sheepswool
sweater with scarlet trimmings, and a child's Tyrolese jacket. I hope they will be appearing shortly.

These newsletters come out in September and March. They are free while current. Back copies 25¢ each.
Each customer receives hers automatically for 2 years from the date of her most recent order. In case
you are interested only in the newsletters, you may order them at the rate of 50¢ per annum.

Well, that about wraps it up until next spring. Sorry I'm a little late this time. It's been a busy
summer, including Europe re-visited after 27 years. The Bohus sweaters from Sweden are magnificent,
both in design and texture. They use occasional P stitches in colour-patterns, with pleasing effect.

Sincerely - Elizabeth

My brother's favorite knitting story:
"One day I needed a ride and my mother drove over to pick me up. She turned onto a one-way street with cars parked along both sides and only a narrow lane open down the middle. As she approached the entrance to a parking lot, a guy pulled out and both cars came to an abrupt halt, nose-to-nose. Someone had to give way. The guy shrugged his shoulders and crossed his arms as if to say, 'I'm not movin', Baby'. My ma reached down, picked up her knitting and, with her hands in plain sight on top of the wheel, placidly started to knit. In a rage, the guy jammed his car into reverse, screeched back into the parking lot and my ma, putt - putt - putt, proceeded down the street."

Elizabeth Zimmermann (signature)

ELIZABETH ZIMMERMANN
Box 157. Babcock. WI 54413

NEWSLETTER #11: 5 CAPS   Fall 1963
(Second, and, it is to be hoped,
improved edition. Fall 1981)   25¢

Dear Knitter, Consider the advantages of knitted headgear. Knitted caps are fast and easy to make (at least, I think mine are). They draw praise and admiration, and use up odds and ends of yarn. They are warm and comfortable to wear and easy to wash. This adds up to pleasant knitting for presents, and excellent profit-making for bazaars.

Here are some good caps, all in Fisherman, Homespun or 2-ply Sheepswool, on a 16" circular needle, at a GAUGE of 5 sts to 1". I take a #5 needle; you may need a different size, depending on your knitting tension. Each cap uses under 1 skein of wool. Put in color patterns if and as you wish. (see Newsletter #2). They can be worked from wool oddments, doubled if thin, or even thribbled, since patterns may well be slightly heavier than the background. For caps with heavier wool at 4 sts to 1" (3-ply Sheepswool or 2-ply Icelandic), cast on 20% less stitches.

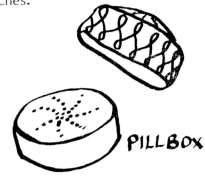

PILLBOX

PILLBOX: Cast on 91 sts. Join. Knit around for ½" for hem. Purl 1 round. K straight for 3½". P 1 round. Shape for top: Decrease 7 sts evenly spaced around (i.e. K 11, K 2 tog around). K 1 round. Repeat these 2 rounds until there are 49 sts. Change to 4 needles, and decrease every round until there are 7 sts left. Finish off. Sew up hem with many loose stitches. (Actually, I recommend you make the hat first, pick up the sts around the bottom edge, knit the hem, and sew the sts down right off the needle, thus providing an elastic edge to the hem. 1981 re-printing note.) Dampen and block over a canister 6" in diameter.

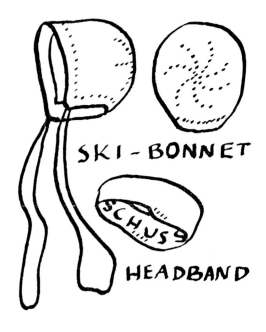

SKI - BONNET

HEADBAND

SKI-BONNET: Totally adjustable; fits all ages. Cast on 77 sts. Join. K 4". Shape top as for Pillbox. To form back of neck, baste a straight line from edge to beginning of decrease. Machine-stitch twice on each side of basting. Cut on basting. With right side toward you, pick up 18 sts along the Right cut edge, 74 sts along front edge, 18 sts along Left cut edge, and 2 sts at center back. K around for 1". P 1 round. K 1". Do NOT cast off, but pull the needle out and sew stitches down on the wrong side forming the hem. Make a 2-yard cord and thread through the hem, knotting it at the back of the neck. Pull out loops at the corners for ties.

HEADBAND: Cast on 90 sts. Join. P 1 round. K ½". Shape for back: K 15, turn. P 30, turn. K 35, turn. P 40, turn. K 45, turn. P 50, turn. K 55, turn. P 60, turn. K for 1½". P 1 round. Change color and work the lining to correspond. Do not cast off, but pull needle out, and weave end cunningly to beginning. You can embellish the lining with fitting thoughts: "Ski-Heil", "Vorlage", "Meister-wedler". Work out the letters 5 squares high on graph paper, and knit them in.

VERY WARM HAT: Reversible. Good for M or F, and wearable as many ways as there are people. Cast on 91 sts. Join. P 1 round. K 6" (or more), and shape top as for Pillbox. For lining, with right side towards you, pick up 91 sts around the edge in a different color, and repeat the process. This is our favorite at the moment.

AND, if anyone still wishes for a FAST CAP, make a Pillbox 5" deep without a hem or a P round, but WITH a ribbed or garter-stitch edge. Leaving 18 sts for back and 37 sts for front, pick up 18 sts for each earflap. Work 1" on these 18 sts, then decrease 1 st at the beginning of each row down to nothing. Make ties of Idiot's Delight (see MARY THOMAS, page 124).

Well, that about wraps it up until next Spring. Sorry I'm a little late this time. It's been a busy summer, including Europe re-visited after 27 years. The Bohus sweaters from Sweden are magnificent, both in design and texture. They use occasional Purl stitches in color-patterns, with very pleasing effect.

Good Knitting—
Elizabeth.

Maura Stone writes: "I was one of the lucky ones to have taken a class from Elizabeth. I drove about 175 miles to get there and walked into the shop where the owner told me that I hadn't registered ahead of time and there wasn't room for me that day. Elizabeth pooh-poohed the owner and told her that she (EZ) could perch on a counter and I could have her chair. Needless to say, it was a wonderful day; I learned so much even though I had been knitting since I was a child. And the most important thing I learned was to write at least one letter or postcard a week to someone expressing my opinion or my praise for something that person said or did. And not necessarily about knitting; she encouraged us to become activists or advocates in our own ways about things that were important to us."

And, from other knitters:

"I made my first EZ sweater in 1968 as I knitted along with the Busy Knitter program on PBS in Omaha, Nebraska ... the first sweater I'd ever made that fit!"

"Listening to EZ, I understood knitting in a new way."

"After hearing about it forever, I finally ordered EZ's 'Knitting Without Tears'. To all of you knitting newcomers, or actually anyone, beginner or expert, who hasn't read it - find a copy today! What a freeing experience ... and a thoroughly enjoyable read, to boot."

"My favorite knitting philosophers are Elizabeth Zimmermann, Meg Swansen, Medrith Glover, Anna Zilboorg, and Debbie New. They all know how to have fun with their yarn."

"Once the light bulb actually goes on, you will never look at one of EZ's patterns with concern again. They are beautiful in their simplicity, with dazzling results."

Pillbox knitted by Jane Lippmann
Baby Surprise Jacket knitted by Lloie Schwartz

knitted by Carol Knott

V. Warm Hat, unlined, with I-Cord bow.

knitted by Renate Baur

Ski-bonnet

E l i z a b e t h   Z i m m e r m a n n

L: knitted by Meg Swansen. R: knitted by Judith Sopher.

Headbands

The Opinionated Knitter

knitted by Meg Swansen.

L and R: the V. Warm Hat, fully lined with negative-image patterns on the reverse side; knitted in 2-ply Unspun Icelandic wool.
Center: a reversible Watch Cap; instructions may be found on page 30

Elizabeth Zimmermann

knitted by Joy Slayton

A Fast Cap (and Tomten Jacket, page 42)

Elizabeth Zimmermann

ELIZABETH ZIMMERMANN
BOX 5555 MILWAUKEE, WIS. 53211

Newsletter and Leaflet #12
Free until Fall '64; then 25¢
Extra copies 25¢.

Dear Knitter,

Your mail asks for a V-necked sweater and classic Aran directions. So I shall combine the two by giving you a drop-shouldered V-necked cardigan with Fishbone and Diamond Aran patterns. If you want a pullover, cut just as far as the V. For a plain sweater, omit the patterns. For a raglan style, you might combine the patterns with leaflet #8. Remember that you are the boss of your knitting, so follow your own desires. The sweater below is 40" around -- a useful size for the whole family. I put ribs between the patterns, so if you want a smaller size, leave out a few of these. In any case, make a cap first, on about 90 sts, using the patterns given. It will serve as a useful swatch. Traditional Arans are always knitted in unbleached Cream wool, but are very acceptable in Oatmeal, and handsome in any colour. I have included directions for the Tree of Life pattern, in case you wish to make borders of this, as the Irish often do.

V-NECKED ARAN CARDIGAN. Size: Medium to large (40" around)

GAUGE. 5 sts. to 1", measured over stocking-stitch.

MATERIALS. 5 skeins 2-ply Sheepswool, or 6-7 skeins Fisherman Yarn. 1 24", 1 16" circular needle, of a size to give you 5 sts. to 1". (I use #5) 4 double-pointed needles of the same size for cuffs. 1 pr. 14" needles two sizes smaller for cardigan border.

ABBREVIATIONS. K 1B. K into back of st. to achieve a twisted stitch. B tw. (Back twist). K into 2nd st. from back, K into 1st st. from front, sl. both sts. off needle together. F tw. (Front twist). K into 2nd st. from front, K into 1st st. from back, sl. both sts. off needle together. "Back twist" and "Front twist" form the "Travelling stitch", which is frequently found in Aran knitting, and is typical of it.

BODY. With 24" needle, cast on 240 sts. Join, being careful not to twist, and establish patterns as follows:- *K 3,P 1,K 1B,P 1,K 1B,P 1, rnd 1 of DIAMOND PATTERN, P 1,K 1B,P 1,K 1B,P 1, rnd. 1 of FISHBONE PATTERN, P 1, K 1B,P 1,K 1B,P 1, rnd. 1 of DIAMOND PATTERN, P 1,K 1B,P 1,K 1B,P 1. Rep from * 3 times for 1st rnd. Continue in patterns as established. When first Diamond is done, you may like to fill succeeding ones with different patterns. I did; using garter-st: stocking-st: quartered stock-ing and reverse stocking-st: seed-st: K 1B,P 1,rib: and K 2 rnds P 2 rnds.

TO SHAPE V-NECK. At 19"(or desired height to underarm), decr. 1 st. each side of centre-front K 3 rib every 2nd rnd, leaving rib intact, and gradually eliminating Diamond on each side, to give a pigeon-chested effect. (This shape will disappear when you cut.) When you have decreased 19 sts. on each side, work straight to shoulder (about 27", or desired height). Cast off fronts, and work back and forth on 120 sts. of back, casting off 10 sts. at the beginning of each row. Place the last 40 sts. on thread or holder.

DIAMOND PATTERN. 14 sts. 26 rnds.
1. *P 6,B tw,P 6.
2. P 6,K 2,P 6.
3. P 5,F tw,B tw,P 5.
4. P 5,K 1,P 2,K 1,P 5.
5. P 4,F tw,P 2,B tw,P 4.
6. P 4,K 1,P 4,K 1,P 4.
7. P 3,F tw,P 4,B tw,P 3.
8. P 3,K 1,P 6,K 1,P 3.
9. P 2,F tw,P 6,B tw,P 2.
10. P 2,K 1,P 8,K 1,P 2.
11. P 1,F tw,P 8,B tw,P 1.
12. P 1,K 1,P 10,K 1,P 1.
13. F tw,P 10,B tw.
14. K 1,P 12,K 1.(Widest point.)
15. B tw,P 10,F tw.
16. Rep rnd 12.
17. P 1,B tw,P 8,F tw,P 1
18. Rep rnd 10
19. P 2,B tw,P 6,F tw,P 2.
20. Rep rnd 8
21. P 3,B tw,P 4,F tw,P 3.
22. Rep rnd 6.
23. P 4,B tw,P 2,F tw,P 4.
24. Rep rnd 4.
25. P 5,B tw,F tw,P 5.
26. Rep rnd 2. Rep from*.

The Loden Green Aran cardigan on page 69 has a different stitch pattern inside each diamond. This was one of Elizabeth's ways to make a textured garment even more interesting to knit.

SLEEVES. With double-pointed needles, cast on 48 sts. Join, and continue around. Establish patterns, with Fishbone at centre, flanked by ribs and Diamonds. Keep 3 K sts, at underarm, and inc. 1 each side of them every 5th rnd. You will soon have enough sts, for the 16" needle. At 18", or desired length, cast off in K and P as pattern dictates.

MAKING-UP. Mark straight armholes at the K 3 ribs at sides of body with basting, to correspond exactly to sleeve-tops. Baste down centre-front. With sewing-machine, using small st, and loose tension, stitch 2 rows each side of basting. Cut on basting; the pigeon-chest will fall into an elegant V. Sew shoulder seams. With 14" needle, pick up 2 sts, for every 3 rnds, up R front, 3 sts, for every 4 rnds, along V, K 40 sts of back, (decreasing them to about 25), and so on down L front. K 4-row band on all sts. Make a 3-st. buttonhole at each Diamond, and continue to K until you have 6 ridges of garter-st. Cast off on the right side, in Purl; it gives an unusually neat edge. (I think I invented this.) Hem sleeve-tops carefully over armholes from the right side. Neaten raw edges inside with herringbone stitch. Block.

```
FISHBONE PATTERN. 9 sts. 4 rnds.
*Rnd 1. sl 3 sts on spare needle and hold in back
of work, K 1, K 3 from spare needle, K 1, sl 1 st
on spare needle and hold in front of work, K 3,
K 1 from spare needle. Rnds 2-4. K 9. Rep from*.

TREE OF LIFE PATTERN. 14 sts. 6 rnds.
1. K 1,K 1B,K 1,P 3,F tw,K 1B,B tw,P 3.
2. K 1,K 1B,K 1,P 3,K 1,P 1,K 1B,P 1,K 1,P 3.
3. K 1,K 1B,K 1,P 2,F tw,P 1,K 1B,P 1,B tw,P 2.
4. K 1,K 1B,K 1,P 2,K 1,P 2,K 1B,P 2,K 1,P 2.
5. K 1,K 1B,K 1,P 1,F tw,P 2,K 1B,P 2,B tw,P 1.
6. K 1,K 1B,K 1,P 1,K 1,P 2,K 1,K 1B,K 1,P 2,K 1,P 1.
7. K 1,K 1B,K 1,F tw,P 1,F tw,K 1B,B tw,P 1,B tw.
Repeat rnds 2 through 7.
```

THOUGHTS AND COMMENT.
If elbows wear thin, make knitted patches of leftover yarn. More fun, and better-looking, than darning.

Paula Simmons, of Suquamish, Wash., handspins magnificent knitting yarn from her own flock of black sheep. Send 25¢ to her for samples, and order, not by colour, but by the actual names of the sheep themselves.

Are you a mail-orderer by temperament? If so, you might like a copy of Elizabeth Squire's "Mail Order Shopping Guide", published last Fall at $1.95. I am gratified to be mentioned in this book, and will gladly send you a copy. Money back, of course, if you don't like it.

Yes, that was me on Beulah Donahue's WTMJ-TV (Milwaukee) programme, for 12 Tuesdays. The ensuing avalanche of mail is one reason for the lateness of this newsletter, and I hope you will forgive me. Happy Summer.

Sincerely

Elizabeth

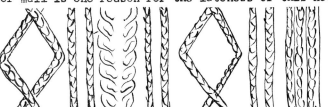

A knitter writes:

"For me, as a teacher and knitter, EZ's single most important contribution was her willingness, eagerness, and wonderful ability to disseminate information. Between her Newsletters, books, Wool Gatherings, and TV series', she reached thousands upon thousands of knitters during a time when knitting wasn't hip or cool or trendy. There was no Amazon.com to look at for 250 knitting books. Her communication style was so encouraging and welcoming. She empowered ('90s buzz word, sorry!) thousands of blind followers to think for themselves."

and from another knitter:

"I have been reading your book on knitting. I find it inspirational like your mother's books. Thanks for providing a wonderful service that we can all enjoy; challenging and enlightening designs, and a great spirit and philosophy for all of us."

knitted by Mary Anderson

Elizabeth Zimmermann

knitted by Meg Swansen

The Opinionated Knitter

The article that follows is one I wrote for the Winter '98/'99 issue of VK; reprinted here by permission of Vogue Knitting International. The sweater shown is the one Elizabeth knitted for the 1958 issue of Vogue Pattern Book.

With Aran sweaters so ubiquitous in recent decades, it is difficult to imagine that the sweater shown here – knitted for *Vogue* in 1958 – was the very first Aran pattern commercially published in the United States … **18**58 would be more believable.

In 1956 Elizabeth had set up a meeting with the *VK* editors to show them a number of her designs. The editors were interested in her garments -

and paid particular attention to the natural, unbleached Sheepswool she had used to knit some of the sweaters. When asked for her source of the wool, Elizabeth suddenly -- and quite uncharacteristically --- became evasive (she later told me that she had surprised herself by her presence-of-mind), at which point the editors excused themselves and disappeared into the back room. They re-emerged and asked if Elizabeth, following a set of instructions they had received from their British office, would knit up a prototype garment for them using her unbleached Sheepswool. She said, "certainly".

After the sweater was finished and sent to the editors, Elizabeth heard nothing further; the matter of a fee had not even been discussed. She was too polite to write or call and simply waited. Eventually the beautiful sweater was published in Vogue Pattern Book (yes, back then a knitting pattern was often included at the end of that sewing magazine) and her copies arrived. Ahhh - **there** was her payment: an editorial mention of her name and address as the source for natural, unbleached wool with which to knit this beautiful Aran sweater. That type of wool was then a great rarity in the US.

The orders and enquiries began flooding in, and the mail-order knitting-

supply business which is now Schoolhouse Press, was born.

In her book, Knitter's Almanac (Dover Publications) Elizabeth remembers the Vogue/Aran story as follows:

Many years ago I was provided with genuine Irish instructions and permitted to make the first Aran sweater I had ever seen or heard of, for Vogue Pattern Book. For this purpose I took unbleached wool and needles with me the next time we went weekend-camping.

Those were the palmy days of camping when firewood and campsites were plentiful and the ranks of the faithful so uncluttered that one was not eternally threading one's way between neighbor's washlines and campfire smoke. We arrived at the Mississippi, set up camp and took to the water, me, of course, with my knitting. All day long, in perfect early-summer weather, we were dandled by the milky ripples of the young but already mighty Miss. I puzzled over the directions which included no picture of what I was actually making; the unaccustomed terms of Back Twist and Forward Twist made themselves gradually at home in my brain, the oiled wool slipped through my fingers, '… the sun beat down upon it all, and thus my dream began.'* Not quite a dream, but a strong feeling that my fingers knew quite well what they were about and welcomed the chance to be about it again after a long lapse of time. I knew then that I had been through this before, with younger fingers in a ruder boat, rocked on the salty summer waves of the Atlantic off the Irish coast. Silly? No.

To design your own Aran, multiply your gauge (in pattern) times wanted circumference and find the total number of body stitches you need. Then plot your design by placing the main motifs (in this case, diamonds and fishbone cables) where you want them on a bird's-eye-view of the sweater. How many stitches did that take? Use up the leftover stitches between the motifs with simple "fillers": for instance, P1, K1b, P1, K1b, P1 makes a pretty little divider

and uses up 5 stitches (or only 3 if you eliminate the final K1b, P1). Stick these units around the garment, nicely balanced, then count it all up to see how close you are to your wanted number of stitches. Add or subtract stitches where necessary.

When working from the lower edge to the shoulder, you may increase the circumference of the sweater gradually, by sneakily inserting another purl stitch each side of the front diamonds; a few

inches further, each side of the back diamonds. If more stitches are wanted, you may repeat the foregoing each side of the Fishbone Cables. The increases are undetectable and your sweater will taper nicely for a broad-shouldered person.**

It was Elizabeth's preference to fill each diamond with a different texture stitch: garter, seed, double-seed, ribbing, travelling stitch, reverse stocking stitch, etc. (see page 69)

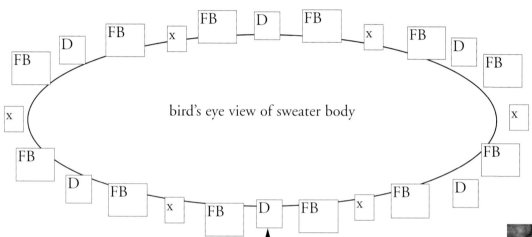

bird's eye view of sweater body

** You may want the shape of a narrow band of "ribbing" around the lower edge, which then blouses up to full body circumference. In that case, sneak in the additional purl stitches *each* side of *each* main motif all in one round for an approximately 10% increase above ribbing.

This schematic is a layout for the "first" Aran shown in the photographs on these two pages. Plan for at least one purl stitch on either side of each FB and D motif.

D = diamond
FB = fishbone
x = a "filler": P1, K1b, P1, K1b, P1, or maybe a small 2-stitch cable with a purl each side, or you could put P1, K1b, P1 between each diamond and fishbone ... anything you like or need to use up all the stitches. *(see text above)*
↑ = center front

*After years of searching, kind knitter Audrey Thorson supplied me with the origin of this quote; from the poem, *Pre-Existence* by Frances Cornford, which Audrey had had to memorize as a schoolgirl in Great Britain.

Elizabeth Zimmermann

ELIZABETH ZIMMERMANN
BOX 5555 MILWAUKEE, WIS. 53211

Newsletter and Leaflet # 13
"ONE & THREE" sweater.
Free until spring '65; then 25¢.
Extra copies 25¢.

Dear Knitter,
          This letter will be rather "show and tell". May I start by recommending a
sweater or cardigan made from the hieroglyphic on the right. At a GAUGE of 5 sts to 1",
212 sts in 2-ply Sheepswool or Fisherman Yarn will give you a sweater 42" around -- a
good size for most adults. For directions use #2 ski-sweater leaflet, or #8 raglan if
you are feeling ambitious. As you work you will begin to see this design's inflexible
logic, for all pattern rounds consist of one stitch of one colour and three of another.
The design is thus satisfying both to knit and to look at. I give alternate colour-
-schemes, and you may of course devise your own, using commercial knitting worsted for
any colour I cannot supply. (TREASON.) Notice the purled stitches, which make the de-
-sign look like pheasant's plumage. This technique is inspired by the Bohus knitting
from Göteborg in Sweden. If you find purling troublesome, you may knit these stitches
instead, and still produce a beautiful sweater.

Now the big news. Gladys Thompson is working on another book of knitting.
The publishers told me in London that it will surpass even "Guernsey and Jersey Patterns"
and that they hope to have it out in fall,1965, so -- patience and fortitude.

In Germany I found some unusual plastic cooking-spoons and also a splendid bunch of ban-
-dannas. The spoons are 10" long, pale blue, square-ended, and hold 5 tsps. (75¢ each)
The bandannas are 30" X 30", of heavy long-fibre cotton and come in deep blue or black
with small white printed pattern and border. They drape well and are good for tying up
your hair or luggage (as the Japanese do) or around your waist for an apron. ($2 each)

In Edinburgh I bought some hand-knitted Tam-o'-Shanters; they have varied Fair Isle
patterns on a natural beige Shetland background. The decreasing-stsr designs are a
sight to be seen, and perhaps to emulate. Small size only, 8½" across.   ($5 each)

You will notice that I have been travelling. Now I am back in the US to find that a
Northern Wisconsin craftsman has wrought me some handsome brass-and-copper buttons.
Made of shell-cases, they take a fine shine, and are right for hunting-jackets, sports-
-clothes and heavy sweaters. For duck-hunting, don't polish. This size)   (50¢ each)

Should you regret having ordered anything from me, return it, and I will refund promptly.

It is a shame that the "new" Gladys Thompson book never materialized - although we remain grateful for her most wonderful *Patterns for Guernseys, Jerseys & Arans* which is in print to this day.

   I found some correspondence between Gladys and Elizabeth and learned that the Guernsey and Jersey book had had the Aran section added on at the last minute. Also, Gladys had originally written the sweater instructions for traditional, circular construction -- but the publisher decided that most British knitters preferred to knit in flat pieces - so all of the patterns were re-written for flat knitting. Sounds strangely familiar, and ... so much for historical accuracy.

Woman's Day has taken several of my designs; a long cherry-coloured scarf-cum-stocking-cap, a tie knitted lengthwise, and ski-headbands. An Aran cardigan will appear there next February. My "Hawser" sweater is on p.44 of McCall's Needlework, winter '64-'65.

Did you ever see anything like this <u>Icelandic Sheepswool?</u> I kept quiet about it until I could import enough. The staples (fibres) are so magnificently long that the yarn isn't spun, just d-r-a-w-n out. So <u>don't wind it</u>; just pull it gently into a smooth box (this is called "nesting"), and knit it gently back out. When knitted this yarn is as strong as any other. Single ply, it makes splendid socks, at a firm 6 sts to 1". For 2 Or 3-ply, nest each ply into its own box, and then combine them by nesting all into yet another. 2-ply at 4 or 4½ sts to 1" gives a lovely useful sweater. 3-ply makes a really thick garment, and 4-ply stands alone. This material is neither for beginners, nor should it be mixed with young children or puppies; it is a rewarding challenge for the experienced knitter, yielding a hairy, strong but silky fabric -- quite beguiling. Each of the five colours is natural sheep and comes in generous 4 oz wheels at $3 a wheel. Four of these are sufficient for an average 2-ply sweater.

This Barn-red is a fine new colour in Fisherman Yarn. Attach it to your sample-card, or send for a new card if your is nibbled at. As sample-cards are a chore to make, I do not scatter them prodigally, but one is yours for the asking.

<u>USEFUL NOTE</u>. I invariably increase by making a backward loop over the right needle. (This method is the same as raising and knitting into the back of the running thread between stitches; Mary Thomas Knitting Book, p.75.) This is the least visible way of increasing, and has the advantage of being a stitch by itself -- a really made stitch. In directions I call it "M 1".

Well, as I said, patience and fortitude in all things. See you in the spring.

Elizabeth

Average "ONE & THREE" sweater in Fisherman Yarn(F) and/or 2-ply Sheepswool(S) takes:

		<u>or</u>	<u>or</u>	<u>or</u>		
4 skeins	Loden(S)	Teal(F)	Oatmeal(S)	Oatmeal(S)		
1 skein	✕ Barn-red(F)	✕ Scarlet(F)	✕ Honey(S)	✕ White(F)	✕	} Purl
"	O Oatmeal(S)	O Light Grey(F)	O Loden(S)	O Black(F)	O	stitches
"	∕ Light Grey(F)	∕ Brown Heather(F)	∕ Cream(S)	∕ Airforce Blue(F)	∕	

I see that the Three & One Sweater was actually called "One & Three". I am uncertain how and why it was switched around, but I have always known it as "Three & One".

Whatever its name, this is one of the most soothing and hypnotic patterns to knit. You quickly fall under the spell of its rhythm and the motif itself appears quite different in varied color combinations.

Two of the photographed sweaters have purl stitches incorporated (pheasant's plumage) and two are plain.

Not wishing to be contradictory, but Elizabeth's M1 is not exactly the same as the raised-running-thread increase. Although they are both twisted loops, M1 is made with the working wool while the Raised Thread increase must borrow wool from the two stitches of the preceding round – which makes the increase snugger and less visible.

Years later, Elizabeth came up with the variation of Knit-into-the-*back*-of-the-stitch-of-the-row-below, which truly is a nearly invisible increase, and, like both the above, can be mirror-imaged beautifully.

both knitted by Elizabeth Zimmermann

Elizabeth Zimmermann

Both cardigans knitted by Meg Swansen

Elizabeth Zimmermann

ELIZABETH ZIMMERMANN
BOX 5555 MILWAUKEE, WIS. 53211

Newsletter and Leaflet # 14
ICELANDIC YOKE-SWEATER.
Free until fall 1965; then 25¢.
Extra copies 25¢.

Dear Knitter,

      In 1958 I prophetically gave you a yoke sweater. They are now so fashionable that I give you another version of it. The basic concept of construction follows in this paragraph; it leaves to you the choice of design, size and yarn. This sweater goes by formula (you will find percentages in parentheses), and up to the underarm is identical with my #4 Brooks and #8 Raglan models. Yoke-shaping is governed by measurement; let us take as an example the sweater given below. The body is 20" across, so the depth of the yoke is 10", i.e. half of body-width. Work 5" of this without shaping, and into the upper 5" fit three decreasing-rounds of K 1, K 2 tog around. Be sure not to start decreasing until the yoke is half-finished. When yoke is 1" shy of desired length, work vital back-of-neck shaping. Neck, cuffs and lower edge may be finished with hem or ribbing. I like to have patterns on the yoke only, but the Icelanders put them on cuffs and lower edge as well.

<u>DIRECTIONS</u> are for a 2-ply Icelandic yoke-sweater, 40" around.
<u>GAUGE</u>. 4 sts. to 1"; 16 sts. to 4"; 160 sts. to 40".
<u>MATERIALS</u>. 4 wheels Icelandic Wool, doubled; 1 wheel for patterns.
    One 24" and one 16" circular needle, one set of sock-needles, approx. size 7 or 8, to give above GAUGE.
<u>BODY</u>. With 24" needle, cast on 160 sts. Join, being careful not to twist. P 1 rnd. for hem. Knit for 17" or to desired length to underarm. Put 12 sts. (approx 8% of 160 sts of body) on thread at each underarm. Set aside and work sleeves.
<u>SLEEVE</u>. Cast on 32 sts. (20% of 160), using sock-needles. Join. P 1 rnd. Work in Knit, increasing 2 sts. at underarm every 5th rnd. Change to 16" needle when practicable. At 54 sts. (approx. 33% of 160) work straight to 18" or to desired length to underarm. Put 12 sts. on thread at underarm. Put all 220 sts. of body and sleeves on 24" needle, matching underarms.
<u>YOKE</u>. K 1½", then work pattern A, changing pattern-rnds. behind L shoulder. Work decr-rnd. as follows:- K 1, K 2 tog. around. (147 sts). Work pattern B. Rep. decr.-rnd. (98 sts). Work pattern C. Rep. decr. rnd. (64 sts. -- 40% of 160.)
<u>SHAPING OF NECK-BACK</u>. Starting at L shoulder, turn, P 32 to R shoulder, turn, K 34, turn, P 36, turn, K 38, turn, P 40, turn. Continue to K for 1" or until yoke measures 10" at the front. P 1 rnd. for hem. K 5 rnds. Next rnd, K 2, make 1, around. K 5 rnds. Do not cast off, but sew hem under, neatly and fairly loosely. Weave underarms. Pick up 160 sts. around lower edge. K 1 rnd, then K 8, K 2 tog. around. (10% decr.) Work 1½" and sew under as on neck. Finish cuffs similarly. (Hems may be worked in thinner yarn.) This is a fine warm seamless sweater that will fit, thanks to cunning hems and neck-shaping, which are Mine Alone.

This issue was published during the height of Icelandic-Yoke-Sweater popularity and the design may also be found in chapter 4 of *Knitting Without Tears*.

    In 1965, most of the commercially available instructions had you Cast Off the underarm stitches on body and sleeves and cobble them together ... most uncomfortable and unelastic. Also, there was no back-of-neck shaping on most of the patterns, which, although reversible front-to-back, produced a pitifully gaping neck-back and a choking neck-front. I believe, in recent years, commercial instructions have altered both of these drawbacks.

    When shaping the neck-back, employ "wrapping" each time (see page 54) to make the turning points invisible.

THOUGHTS AND COMMENT. Let us step right under the cold shower and get the bad news over with. For the first time, my prices are going up. I held out as long as I could, but profits were dwindling, and we can't have that. So as of July 1st 1965 each skein will cost 15¢ more. Sheepswool, $1.35. Sheepsdown and Fisherman Yarn, $1.65. "Homespun", $1.95. Icelandic Wool still $3 a wheel. No increase on tweeds needles or books. And talking of books reminds me; I have found two wowsers:-

MARIANNE KINZEL's "First Book of Lace Knitting" and "Second Book of Lace Knitting" are published in England. The variety and Austrian elegance of her patterns make them totally fascinating. I immediate--ly thought of fine yarns and gossamer shawls, of cool summer shells in linen or cotton. Mrs Kinzel gives detailed instructions as well as explicit charts. Each book, $5. Money-back guarantee, of course.

TIENS! I won a prize in Paris in the "Jardin des Modes" Championnat de Tricot. I entered a ski-sweater, which will appear in a newsletter one day, maybe. My new Aran ("Fools-in-the-River") was in the Feb 1965 Woman's Day, but watch out; directions are for straight needles. Woman's Day has also taken five pairs of ski-stockings, designed from quite a new angle. So keep looking for these, faithful knitters.

MAILING-LIST is restricted to those who send in at least one yarn order every 2 yrs. After this I reluctantly but ruthlessly deposit you in the sleeping-file. (Otherwise I would be addressing envelopes all year; I still refuse to have this done mechanically.) You may subscribe to the newsletters only for $1 every two years -- 4 issues.

IDEAS for the subject of next fall's newsletter are invited. A knitting-book will be the lovely reward for the first one of you to suggest the subject I ultimately use. (Do not include baby-clothes.)

KIND DEED DEPT. Mrs Eloise Forrer (Alakanuk, ALASKA.) runs a knitting-class for Eskimo girls. They need yarn. Why don't you send along any that you <u>don't</u> need? Mail to her; or to me, and I will forward.

MAGIC THIMBLES FROM GERMANY, small, med. or large. 25¢ each if included with yarn order. Otherwise 35¢.

BUTTONHOLES. I have a solution for these tiresome things. It concerns 3 rows. <u>ROW 1</u>. Cast off 3 sts. <u>ROW 2</u>. cast on 3 by the primitive method of making 3 backward loops over the R needle. <u>NOW</u>, pick up the first st you cast off in the previous row, put it on L needle, K 2 tog. <u>ROW 3</u>. When you come to the 3 cast-on sts, K into the back of each, and for good measure into the back of the next st. That's all. I think you will find that you have tightened up those sloppy corners.

Sincerely Elizabeth

Elizabeth writes:

I am sitting here by the river, the portable typewriter on a makeshift table and a picnic basket stashed in the shade.

.... After our picnic, we took knitting and fishpole and paddled slowly upstream, passing the landmarks in reverse: Ninka's Wallow, the Wolfsschlucht, the sandbank and on up to another sandbank where the canoe sighed softly to shore.

The Old Man took his rod and went to work, although the wind was from the East (fish bite least) and I knitted my way through the woods, ankle-deep in Spring Beauties.

Do I miss the English Primroses, Bluebells, Speedwell and Pimpernel? Yes, of course. But the English have no Spring Beauties, Trillium, Dogtooth Violets or Bloodroot except in a pleasant but rather elliptical poem by Kipling. Compensations must be faced squarely and with appreciation.

Both adult cardigans knitted by Lois Young.; child's pullover knitted by Alison Albrecht

Q: "At the end of one of Elizabeth Zimmermann's fine videos there is a very amusing vignette in which she is busted for knitting without a license – while a passenger on the back of a motorcycle! Please tell us more about this funny scene."

A: Well, since you ask.... Elizabeth and her husband rode BMW motorcycles for many decades - until they were well into their eighties. They even motored to the East coast once, where Elizabeth gave a few workshops without any props (no room on the cycle). She called it her, *Have Mouth, Will Travel* tour.

Elizabeth's last book, Knitting Around, is subtitled, Knitting Without a License, and as we were taping the accompanying video for PBS, my husband decided to stage a little story. We called the one and only policeman in our nearby town and asked if he would like to be in our video. He took it quite seriously and ordered a new cop-cap; shined up his cop-car, etc.

Elizabeth Zimmermann

Elizabeth editing an issue of Wool Gathering. (I-Cord glasses-holder)

We shot footage of Elizabeth in her usual motorcycle mode: sitting and happily knitting behind Gaffer, with a long strand of the wool flying out behind her. The siren went off.

The cycle pulled to the side of the road as the squad car came up behind them.

The policeman got out and walked slowly toward them (in his shiny new boots) and said, "What do you think you're doing?"

Elizabeth: "Why, just Knitting Around, Officer."

Cop: "Do you have a license for that?"

Elizabeth gasped and put her hand to her mouth. Freeze frame.

Q: "Do you mean Elizabeth actually knitted while she was a motorcycle passenger? That's delightful!"

A: Yes. For several years she knitted in secret (my father would not have approved; she was to concentrate on motor-cycling and LEAN into the curves, etc), and used a small circular needle (socks or mittens) in order to keep the knitting in her pocket until they were under way; then she leaned back slightly so Gaffer couldn't feel the movement of her hands.

On the Interstate one day, they were slowly passing a semi and my father happened to see the truck driver laugh and point out my mother's knitting to his passenger. Whoops - found out.

Elizabeth Zimmermann

ELIZABETH ZIMMERMANN
BOX 5555   MILWAUKEE, WIS. 53211

Newsletter and Leaflet # 15
MITTENS
Free until spring 1966; then 25¢.
Extra copies, 25¢

Dear Knitter,   Reprinted by permission of WOMAN'S DAY MAGAZINE, a Fawcett publication.

Men's, Women's, and Children's Mittens—
*Same Directions,
Different Yarn and Needles*

GAUGE: Man's mittens 4 sts = 1″; 6 rows = 1″. **Woman's mittens:** 9 sts = 2″; 11 rows = 2″. **Child's mittens:** 11 sts = 2″; 7 rows = 1″.

NOTE: All sizes are made exactly alike; the differences are achieved by change in yarn and needles. For unbleached sheepswool (which was used for these mittens), write for sample cards to: Elizabeth Zimmerman, 2010 East Wood Place, Milwaukee 11, Wisconsin. When using this yarn, use 4 [3–2] ply wool, needles No. 6 [5–3] (English needles No. 7 [8–10]). ✗ SHEEPSWOOL.

RIGHT MITTEN: Starting at cuff, cast on 36 sts, dividing 16 sts on first needle and 10 each on 2nd and 3rd needles. Work in ribbing of k 3, p 1 for 2″ [1½″–1¼″]. **Next rnd:** (K 2, sl 1, k 1, psso) 9 times (27 sts). K 1″ [¾″–½″] even. **Next rnd:** (K 2, inc 1 st in next st) 9 times (36 sts). **Following rnd:** (K 3, p 1) 4 times; k around. Repeat last rnd until mitten measures 5½″ [5″–4½″] from beg.

Thumb Marking: 1st rnd: Work across first needle in rib pattern. **2nd rnd:** K 3, k 7 with a contrasting thread. Transfer 7 sts just knitted back onto left-hand needle and knit again with working thread. 3rd needle: K across. Keeping first needle in rib pattern and knitting across other 2 needles, work even until mitten measures 10″ [8½″–7″] from beg.

To Shape Tip: Transfer 3 sts from 2nd needle onto first needle. **1st rnd:** 1st needle: K 1, sl 1, k 1, psso, p 1, (k 3, p 1) 3 times; k 2 tog, k 1. 2nd needle: K 1, sl 1, k 1, psso, k across. 3rd needle: K to within last 3 sts, k 2 tog, k 1. **2nd rnd:** K around. Continue decreasing 4 sts in this manner every other rnd until 20 sts remain. Break thread, leaving 8″ end. Weave tip tog, using Kitchener stitch (See General Directions).

Thumb: Remove colored thread. Pick up the 14 lps around opening, and 1 more lp, dividing them on 3 needles. K even for 2½″ [2″–1¾″]. **To Shape Tip:** K 1, ° k 2 tog. Repeat from ° around. Break off, leaving 6″ end. Pull yarn through remaining sts.

LEFT MITTEN: Work as for right mitten to thumb marking. **Thumb Marking:** Work first and 2nd needles in established pattern. 3rd needle: K 3, k 7 onto separate thread as for right mitten. Complete as for right mitten.

As you see, mittens won, hands down. My design above is from Woman's Day Big Book of Knitting, now quite out of print. I have added directions for what I call "Fern-frond" tips (published here for the first time), which are fun to knit and conform well to the hand. And they are cute. It's high time something interesting happened to mittens.

I thank all of you who so kindly sent in suggestions. Mrs Edgar Sommer was the first to suggest mittens, so "First Book of Modern Lace Knitting" goes to her, and I hope she and her knitters have as much fun with it as I am having. I am now on my sixth shawl, using Icelandic wool at single ply, and directions just as they come in the book. These shawls and stoles are soft, warm, light, and lovely. With a 10½ needle and 2 wheels of wool I can make one 48″ across.

I have some splendid Icelandic sheepskins at $20 apiece. The "fur" is all of 8″ long, and they come in snow-white, pitch-black, and an indescribable shade combining cream, grey, and blacksheep. You can make parkas or woolly hats of them, use them as bedroom rugs, wall-hangings, or just something to curl your toes up under in unfriendly weather. Or send them back to me if they fail to charm completely. They will show you why Icelandic wool is so beautiful.

26″
40″

This fall I am having my own television programme over Milwaukee's Channel 10 (WMVS-TV). In a series of 10 half-hours, starting Sept 14th, I shall take you quite discursively through the making of a classic raglan seamless sweater, entirely on circular needles. Times are 3 p.m. on Tuesdays, with repeat at 7.30 p.m. on Thurs. I am working on 10 study-guides, covering the details of each half-hour, and it is a heady pleasure for the writer of knitting directions not to have to condense, eliminate, or abbreviate.

Gladys Thompson's new book is not ready yet - alas - but there is a bran-new edition of "Norwegian Knitting Designs" just out, with chatty and explicit directions for making two typical Norwegian sweaters. The price is up to $4, but it is well worth it.

Embroidery: Starting at cuff edge with contrasting color, & following photograph, work chevron every 3rd row down 3 ribs on back of mitten.

ALTERNATIVE CURLED MITTEN-TIPS.
Starting at *, on 1st needle, K 8, sl 1, K 2 tog, psso, complete rnd. Next rnd, K 7, sl 1, K 2 tog, psso, complete rnd. Next rnd, K 6, sl 1, K 2 tog, psso, complete rnd. Continue thus until 1 st is left on 1st needle. Slip it on to 2nd needle, and weave sts on 2nd and 3rd needle together.

Sincerely Elizabeth.

IN SEPTEMBER "WOMENS DAY" THE YELLOW CAP ON PAGE 49 IS MINE.

TO WEAVE STOCKING-STITCH. Directions are in any knitting-book; here is the way I remember it:-
Have same amt of sts on two needles, wrong sides together. The one nearest you is FRONT NEEDLE; the other one is BACK NEEDLE. Thread blunt weaving-needle with matching yarn. With it....
*Go into the 1st st on FRONT NEEDLE from FRONT. Slip st on to weaving-needle.
 Go into the 2nd st on FRONT NEEDLE from BACK. Leave st on, and pull yarn through both sts.
 Go into the 1st st on BACK NEEDLE from BACK. Slip st on to weaving-needle.
 Go into the 2nd st on BACK NEEDLE from FRONT. Leave st on, and pull yarn through both sts.
Repeat from *. Don t try to keep weaving tidy; just be sure it's accurate. You can always adjust the tension afterwards. Mary Thomas shows woven ribbing. Look it up under "grafting".

Try a pair of Curled Tip Mittens, shown at far right. This design of Elizabeth's is totally unique in the annals of historic and traditional mittens. When you slip them on, they feel like old friends, as they follow the natural curl of your fingers.

L knitted by Elizabeth. R knitted by Linda Lutz

Knitted by Meg Swansen

A Knitting Summit, L to R: Mary Walker Phillips, Elizabeth and
Barbara G. Walker, meeting at Barbara's house in 1980.
(photos T.S. Zimmermann)

Elizabeth Zimmermann

Elizabeth writes:

It has been one of our better Easters. The winter is almost over and gone and the snowdrops will be up soon. Some stubborn and shabby snow lingers in the shade and the river is down. Last night we dyed Easter eggs -- about 1-1/2 dozen of them -- and we changed our technique once again.

Our medium is vegetable dye, which was bought many years ago in a package of four small plastic bottles of red, blue, yellow and green. I rarely use them during the year unless I'm cooking something which really ought to have more eggs or cheese in it -- then I reach for the yellow, sly old woman that I am. Red is nice for frosting or for cheering up dull applesauce. For blue there is no earthly use that I can think of, but once I used the green in a batch of bread for Saint Patrick's Day. Not a success.

For this year's egg-coloring we put drops of colors in the bottoms of four schnapps glasses and went to work. If you take a very small drop of strong color on the point of a knitting needle, transfer it to the egg and scritch about in it, it is surprising what you can come up with as long as the original blob remains liquid. You can even dilute it a bit if you wish. You can put two blobs, say red and yellow close together and mingle them up -- very creative (!) You can hardly go wrong.

Before long I became very messy, dipped a finger in color and swirled it around the egg until it ran out, becoming paler in the process. Then I took a felt-tipped pen -- a brown one, it happened to be -- and drew little squiggles around the edges of my finger-painting.

In the meantime the Old Man was doing some of his famous funny faces, trees, the Bun and all the things he is so good at. We had a fine collection. To them we added the onion-skin-dyed eggs.

The Easter Stollen was baked and the eggs were dyed, so we took our habitual Saturday evening trip to the Sportsmen's Bar.

After several Babcocktails (cranberry juice and Vodka) we were primed for egg-laying. Luckily there was a moon and we could turn out the yard light, which makes too many deep shadows for successful laying. The Old Man took the South side of the yard and I took the North. He started at the East and I at the West so we couldn't spy on each other. We were soon through and stumbled contentedly into bed.

This morning was perfect; sunny, warm, like nothing we had seen for the last six months and off we sped with our baskets at the ready. We had nine eggs each to find and were neck and neck right up to the end, when the Old Man was floored by one that I couldn't even remember laying. By following my mental processes of the night before I finally caught a glimpse of it, nested in a stunted cedar which is slowly winning its battle with the deer. I guided him to it by the time-honored method of warmer, colder, very warm, boiling hot, scorching, until at last he spotted it. Back into the house, then, to the smell of coffee and a breakfast of our booty, ably backed up by my freshly baked Stollen with pecans.

There was an Easter book at each plate so we spent a happy idle morning reading outside in the sun, had some more breakfast for lunch and raked the grass in the afternoon. For supper, pheasant from the freezer, some of the hoarded wild rice and a bottle of hock; my word, who lives better than we do?

Through the day, the birds had given it all they had, the sun had shone, the clouds gathered, the evening drew in early, rumblings approached and SPLAT SPLAT, huge drops of rain fell. Rain? We haven't seen rain since last November. Truly the winter has had it.

And if you think we are old fools for playing Easter Egg in the snow like little kids, try it yourselves when you get to be sixty.

Elizabeth Zimmermann

ELIZABETH ZIMMERMANN
BOX 157 BABCOCK, WISCONSIN 54413

Newsletter and leaflet #16
Eight unusual knitting techniques
Free until fall 1966; then 25¢.
Extra copies, 25¢.

Dear Knitter,

      Here follow 8 unusual knitting techniques -- not out of conceitedness, but because many have suggested that I combine them in one newsletter. If I won't write a book, that is; and I won't. None of them are to be found in "Mary Thomas's Knitting Book", which means that they must be rare, indeed, although probably not unique. 6 and 7 are bran-new; I know, as I invented them last fall.

<u>1. JOINING FIRST RND ON A CIRCULAR NEEDLE</u>. Work first 3 sts. with the yarn proper and with the tail left over from casting-on. When sweater is finished, this is one end you won't have to fasten off.

<u>2. INCREASING</u>. Increases are usually made in pairs, one each side of 2 or 3 sts. which are left undisturbed. For each inc., make a backward loop over the R needle. In next row, K loops like regular sts. This way is <u>not</u> new, but less well-known than it should be. Try increasing at beg. of row by making a backward loop over the L needle and knitting firmly into it.

<u>3. MITRED CORNERS</u> on cardigans where neck and front sts are picked up in one fell swoop. Mark 1 st. at corner and inc. 1 st. (✗) each side of this every 2nd row. For inside corners, sl. 1, K 2 tog, pass slipped st over (↑) at exact corner every 2nd row

<u>4. BUTTONHOLE</u>. This is worked over 3 rows, and has no sloppy corners.
Row 1. Cast off 3 sts. (or as many as desired, but 3 is usual).
Row 2. Cast on 3 sts. by making 3 backward loops over R needle. NOW, pick up
    first cast-off st. from previous row and put it on L needle. K 2 tog.
Row 3. K into back of 3 cast-on sts. and also into back of next st.

<u>5. AFTERTHOUGHT POCKETS</u>. When garment is done, mark where you want pockets. Snip 1 st. at centre of pocket-line, and unravel in both directions to desired width. Pick up resulting sts. on sock-needles and work around for desired length, purling front sts. on 1st. rnd. Tuck in, fold flat, and weave or sew together. Neaten corners with ravelled yarn.

<u>6. NEAT UNDERARM FOLDLINES ON STOCKING-ST. SWEATER</u> may be made after work is finished, but not cast off. Drop seam-st. clear down to within 2 rows of lower edge. With crochet--hook, hook it up again, taking alternately a single thread and 2 threads together. ⟶ This is great fun to do, works like magic, and makes for easy folding.

Ha! to that second sentence in the first paragraph. **And**, use of the word, "invented".

#2. A few years later, Elizabeth began to mirror-image all paired increases: twist the first loop in one direction and the second in the other; if you do this, knit into the back of the one on the left when next you meet.

#4. Elizabeth's One Row buttonhole in *Knitter's Almanac* and *Knitting Workshop* has superceded this version, as follows: *slip 1 st p'wise. Wool fwd and leave it there. Sl 1 p'wise. Pass 1st sl-st over 2nd. Sl 1 p'wise. Pass 2nd sl-st over 3rd. Sl 1 p'wise. Pass 3rd sl-st over 4th. Put 4th st on L needle, reversing it. Turn last st on R needle. Pull wool tightly and lay it over R needle from front to back. Pass turned st over it. Make 4 firm backward loops over R needle. K 2 tog. Knit to next buttonhole site & repeat from asterisk.

#7. This excellent Cast Off is (with the exception of Tubular Cast Off) the most elastic one I know and is wonderful for from-the-toe socks and necklines. It is particularly beautiful on garter-stitch.

E l i z a b e t h   Z i m m e r m a n n

7. SEWN CASTING-OFF. This has a mild disadvantage, in that it will not unravel. But it is a good addition to your knitting repertoire, and is very elastic, if you don't pull it tight. It looks mysterious and elegant on garter-st.; on stocking-st. it has the great advantage of not curling. For ribbing, not really suitable. Work as follows:- Break off yarn at respectable length, and thread through nice blunt needle. With this needle *go through first 2 sts. from R to L from the back(A). Pull yarn through. Now go through the first st. only, from L to R from the back(B), and take st.off needle. Pull yarn through. Repeat from *.

8. SEAMLESS SWEATERS FROM THE BOTTOM UP, as in newsletters 4,8 and 14. Up to the underarm you work on 3 pieces separately; the body in the living-room (sounds like a whodunit), one sleeve in the car, and the other in your bag. This saves time and frustration. When you join the pieces, the excitement begins, shoulder-shaping starts, rnds become shorter and shorter, and the whole method is psychologically sound. On the other hand, if you are knitting for children, who will grow, and eventually need lengthened sleeves, etc., by all means work from the neck down, but underarms will have to be sewn, and towards the end you will feel as if you are knitting on a octopus.

TELEVISION NOTES. My knitting series last fall on Milwaukee's Educational Channel 10 was a success, and will be re-run, starting March 15th. Tues at 7 pm,right before Julia, and repeat on Wed at 3 pm. (You who carry weight with TV stations in your area may like to know that the video-tapes are for rent. Write to WMVS-TV, 1015 N 6th St, Milwaukee, Wis.53203, or to me.) I made 10 Study Guides to take you in detail through the construction of a seamless classic raglan sweater or cardigan. They were so popular that I am keeping them in print. 25¢ each (to yarn customers, $2 a set of 10):-
1. Casting on, knitting, purling, GAUGE.
2. Starting your sweater.
3. Sleeves and increasing.
4. Assembling body and sleeves
5. Shoulder-shaping and decreasing.
6. Neck-shaping and hems.
7. More about hems, preparing to cut, weaving.
8. Cutting, picking up stitches.
9. Borders, buttonholes, spacing buttonholes.
10. Blocking and finishing.

BOASTING DEPT. I had three sweaters in Wis.Designer-Craftsmen Exhibit 1965. One Honorable Mention.

NOW, SOME COMMERCIALS, unpaid and unsolicited, of course, and highly recommended:-
MEG SWANSEN, our daughter, has her Knitting Workshop at 160 S. Main, in New Hope, Pa. 11 - 2, or by appointment. Tel.862-2142. She carries my wools, and has a pile of her and my sweaters for you to mull over. She manufactures and sells the Country Buttons, which you can also find at Wanamakers.
CAROL BROWN, of course, at Putney, Vt. Handwoven Irish tweeds, Arans, Kinsale cloaks, etc.
SCHAAL YARN CO., 2207 Lowry Ave N, M'polis, Minn. Mr Schaal sews in sleeves in a marvellous fashion.
YARN DEPOT, 545 Sutter St, San Francisco, California. A woolly paradise for weavers and knitters.

#16. All rights reserved.
If you wish to quite, ask me.

Sincerely Elizabeth.

"Boasting Department" (above): it was for that event that Elizabeth designed and knitted "The Hanging" that she describes in an interview at the end of the *Knitting Glossary* video/dvd series. That major annual exhibit had excluded knitting for years, but Elizabeth persevered and eventually broke through to have her pieces accepted in 1958, 1960 and nearly every year thereafter through the above-mentioned in 1965. More about it on the following pages...

Elizabeth at the 1960 Milwaukee Designer-Craftsman Show *(see NL#5 on page 31)*. She is wearing a Sheepsdown Watch Cap *(page 31)* and an Aran cardigan *(page 63)*. The middle sweater and the hooded jacket on the right are knitted with Sheepsdown. The sweater on the left was subsequently re-designed *(see opposite page)* in lighter weight black and white wool with red facings and was published on the cover of McCall's Needlework FW '59-'60 .

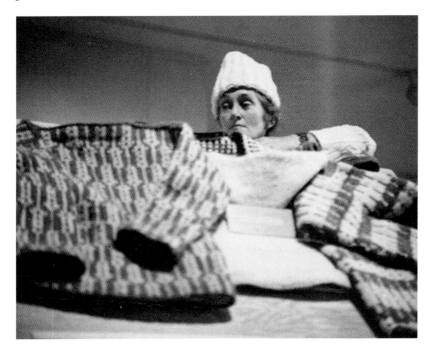

1960, Elizabeth writes:

... studied and travelled in all Western European countries except the Iberian Peninsula, Denmark and Norway.
... With the exception of the first six years of life, knitted continuously and evolved simple method of making Norwegian sweaters in 1955. Like all inventions, it had been already done, but of this I was ignorant. Sold an article and two sweaters to Woman's Day, and with the knitting needles now firmly between my teeth, continued to this day to sell sweater designs to magazines and yarn outfits. Started offering natural wool by mail-order as a sideline and this has now developed into a major hobby.

Had a sweater accepted by the Milwaukee Designer-Craftsmen show in 1958 and emboldened by this, submitted five more sweaters to the Crafts show at the WI State Fair 1959; four accepted. Slight setback at 1959 Designer-Craftsmen Show; all rejected but consoled by theory that I am (as far as I know) the only knitter ever to enter her - or his - work in a show of this kind.

I have a knitting creed slowly developing; roughly as follows: There is enormous potential for genuine creative knitting on the level of any other honest craft. Design in colour can be incorporated in endless combinations and patterns, as well as variations of basic lace designs which have yet to be explored and I am tempted to branch into this field too, as the technique is fascinating and beguiling.

Woven goods are flat and the designer quite rightly cringes at the thought of cutting into the material to make it wearable.

Knitting can be shaped at the edges or in volume, enabling the fabrication of a literally seamless garment, or else one that does not imply cutting out and throwing bits away.

Perhaps one of the most delightful aspects of this simple and ancient craft lies in its employment of the most rudimentary tools -- wool and two sticks; or in the case of circular knitting, only one needle. It can be taken any-where, stuffed into a bag or pocket and the plain bits may be worked in the charming company of friends, sitting or

Joan Schrouder's version of the McCall's cover-sweater

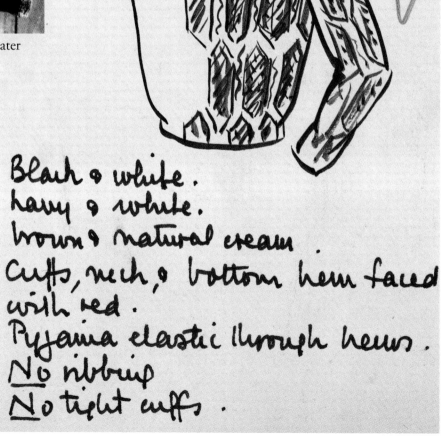

Black & white.
navy & white.
brown & natural cream.
Cuffs, neck, & bottom hem faced
with red.
Pyjama elastic through hems.
No ribbing
No tight cuffs.

waiting in the car, or at any time when one wishes to idle while preserving an appearance of busy industry. The ivory tower may be used when actually designing a pattern or putting in a yoke on a plain sweater -- no two yokes need ever be alike.

Once the design is more or less established comes the satisfying period of physical creation, watching it grow between the fingers.

As each garment is finished comes the sadness of parting, soon assuaged by the casting on of stitches for the next. And how comforting to be engaged in the creation of artifacts for which the demand is — as far as I can see — infinite.

Elizabeth Zimmermann
LTD.

ELIZABETH ZIMMERMANN
BOX 5555 MILWAUKEE, WIS. 53211

Newsletter and leaflet #17
LEGGINGS.   Fall '66
Free until spring '68; then 25¢.
Extra copies, 25¢

Dear Knitter,

Is there a demand for Nether Garments? Longies? Sweaters-from-the-waist-down? If so, I am about to fill it. There is actually less work and material in a pair of tights than in a sweater. They are made in nice soothing circular knitting, with just enough shaping to keep you inter--ested. They are an excellent winter complement to the current abbreviated clothes. They can dash to the store on cold mornings. Skaters and ballet dancers love them. They slip on and off easily for going to the office or to parties. And they are seamless. Make the first pair for the baby, to get the hang of them. These are best made from the waist down, as they fit diapers better, and it is easier to re-foot, or to lengthen them.

BABY LEGGINGS. GAUGE, 5 sts to 1"; 15 sts to 3", etc., (very IMPORTANT). Materials. 2 skeins Fisherman Yarn, 16" circular needle, size 5, or size to give you 5 sts to 1". Set of sock-needles of the same size. Cast on 88 sts. on 16" needle. Work around in rib of K2, P2, for 3 rnds. Next rnd, K2, yarn over, P2 tog around for eyelets. Rib 6 more rnds. Shape back:- Starting at centre-back, K5, turn, P10, turn, K15, turn, P20, turn. Continue thus until you have P40, turn. Work even in stocking-st for 28 rnds. Mark 3 sts at centre-back and -front. Shape for hip:- Inc 1 st each side of marked sts every 3rd rnd. After 10 increase rows (128 sts), work even for 5 rnds. Put 5 sts at centre-back and -front on holders. Complete legs separately on sock-needles. Right Leg:- Work around on 59 sts and dec 2 sts at inseam every 3rd rnd (K2 tog, K1, sl 1, K1, psso)*** At 45 sts work even for 20 rnds. Mark centre-back and dec 2 sts at this point every 3rd rnd until 35 sts remain. Work even for 15 rnds, or to desired length to ankle. Work a foot (Leaflet #10), or make Bootee-foot:- On 13 sts at centre-front make instep. Row 1. sl 1, K11, P1. Row 2. sl 1, K2, P7, K2, P1. Rep these 2 rows 10 times. Pick up 11 sts along sides of this piece and continue around in stocking-st for 10 rnds. On last rnd K2 tog 3 times at toe and heel. Take out needles, fold flat, and weave sides tog. Or you can cast off and sew together if you like. Make Left Leg to correspond. Weave crotch. *** for cute shorts, cast off after 5 rnds.

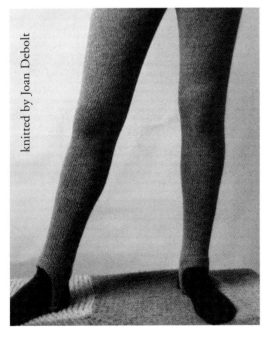

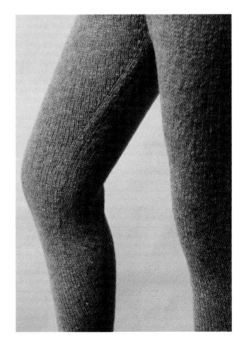

Elizabeth Zimmermann

LADY LEGGINGS. GAUGE, 5 sts to 1"; 15 sts to 3", etc. Best made from ankles up.
Materials. 4 skeins Fisherman Yarn, 1 16", 1 24" circular needle, size 5 or size to give you 5 sts to 1". Set of sock-needles, same size. Take some measurements, and fill out blanks below. You know how sizes vary.

Ankle .... inches		.... sts, called hereinafter A sts.
Knee .... inches	Multiply by	.... sts, called hereinafter K sts.
Thigh .... inches	your GAUGE of	.... sts, called hereinafter T sts.
Hips .... inches	5 sts to 1"	.... sts, called hereinafter H sts.
Waist .... inches		.... sts, called hereinafter W sts.

Is that clear? I hope so. Be sure to have your GAUGE accurate. (If you use different yarn your GAUGE may be different but the formula will still hold.)
Start at Ankle with sock-needles. Cast on A...sts plus 24 sts. Work around in garter-st(K 1 rnd, P 1 rnd), decreasing 2 sts,(sl.1, K2 tog, psso) each side, diametrically opposed, every 2nd rnd, until you have A...sts. This gives a good point at each ankle. You can omit it by casting on A...sts and working 14 rnds in garter-st. Work even in stocking-st to beg. of Calf. about 5". Mark 3 sts at centre-back, and inc.1 st each side of these every 3rd rnd until you have K...sts. Change to 16" needle. Work even to Knee, about 5½". Mark 3 sts at inseam, directly in line with ankle-point, and inc.1 st each side of these every 3rd rnd until you have T...sts. Work even to intersection of legs,about 2", or to desired length. Make another leg. Subtract half of H...sts from T...sts. The difference... (about 10 sts.) is put on holders at inseams for crotch. Join legs by working around on all H...sts on 24" needle for 10 rnds. Shape for Waist:- Mark centre-back and -front, and dec.2 sts(K2 tog, K1,sl 1 psso) at these points every 3rd rnd until you have W...sts. Shape Waist-Back:- Put 1/4 of W...sts on holder at centre-front, and work back and forth on remaining 3/4 of W...sts, leaving 1 st on needle at end of each row, thus working on progressively less sts, leaving the others waiting on needle. When you are down to last 1/4 of W...sts, work around on all sts (incl.those left behind, and those on holder) for 14 rnds of K2, P2, rib. Next rnd, K2, yarn over, P2 tog around for eyelets. Rib 3 more rnds. Cast off loosely. Weave crotch. Sew wide elastic between ankles. Put elastic through eyelets.

"The Busy Knitter"(me) is on these TV stations, for 10 weeks, starting on the following dates:-

Sept 4th KDPS Des Moines, Ia.	Sept 18th WDSE Duluth, Minn.	Oct 16th KUON Lincoln, Neb.
Sept 18th KTCA M'polis, Minn.	Sept 25th WQED Pittsburgh, Pa.	Jan 1st '67 WNMR Marquette, Mich
Sept 18th KTCA St Paul, Minn.	Oct 2nd KUSD Vermilion, SD.	March 5th '67 KFME Fargo, ND.

German Wool-Needles,(Smyrnanadeln); nice and fat; blunt or sharp; 10¢ each. Or 3 for 25¢.

The Wisconsin Institute,1235 N. Milwaukee St, M'kee, has classes in Creative Stitchery, Drawing, Rosemaling, and Watercolour, starting Sept 26th. I shall have my knitting class there, from 1.30 to 3.30 on Wednesdays, every week. For details, telephone me at 962-5376.

Carol Brown, Putney, Vt.05346, has handwoven Irish tweeds & blankets, Arans, intriguing cottons & silks.

McCall's beautiful new Needlework Treasury has two of my early sweaters on pp.232-235. Need I say that the child's sweater was designed for circular needles and cut armholes? And I now weave the underarms of the adult sweater.

The Wisconsin Designer Craftsmen Traveling Exhibit includes two of my sweaters. It will be in Eau Claire, Oshkosh, Lawrence College, Kenosha, and Milwaukee Vocational School between now and March '67

Well now, have a good winter. Knit some longies and keep your legs warm; its half the battle. Sincerely, Elizabeth.

For the Lady Leggings — adjust the number of short rows you put across the waist-back, according to need.

Elizabeth Zimmermann LTD.

ELIZABETH ZIMMERMANN
BOX 5555 MILWAUKEE. WIS. 53211

Newsletter and leaflet #18
STOCKINGS.   Spring '67.
Free until fall '67; then 25¢.
Extra copies, 25¢.

Dear Knitter,

      Stockings are only overgrown socks. (See leaflet #10) The upper part is about 1/3 wider than the ankle, and you can calculate the number of sts. by multiplying these widths by your GAUGE. Distance from knee to ankle is usually about 12", and is divided into 3 equal parts. The middle section is shaped. Fill in your own GAUGE, measurements, and number of sts. → Directions below are for thick stockings in Sheepswool or Icelandic wool with a 12" leg, plus a 4" turnover. Skiers turn this up and anchor it with the lower edge of their knickers. Use K2, P2 rib, which is classic and elegant, or stocking-st with one of the patterns given. "Norwegian Knitting Designs"($4) has scores of designs. Or use cables, allowing a few extra sts, as cables "take up". Run a cable or special pattern down the back; decrease each side of this for a shapely & dashing calf.

> GAUGE...sts. to 1"
> calf......inches.
> ankle.....inches.
> Cast on GAUGE multiplied by calf measurement.......sts.
> Decrease to GAUGE multiplied by ankle measurement...sts.

STOCKINGS. GAUGE: 4 sts. to 1". SIZE: Man's Medium.

Materials: 3 skeins 3-ply Sheepswool or 2 wheels Icelandic wool used double. 1 set #7 needles, or size to give you above GAUGE. Nylon "Heel-N-Toe" for strengthening.

START AT TOP: Cast on 56 sts. Divide on 3 needles, join, and work around in K2, P2 for 4". Change to stocking-st.(all K). Work 4". SHAPE CALF: Mark 2 sts. (or more) at centre-back, and decr. 1 st each side of these every 4th rnd.until you have 44 sts. Work even until piece measures 16" or to desired length.

HEEL FLAP: Work on 22 sts. of back only. Join in nylon.
Row 1:sl 1, K20, P1, turn. Row 2:sl 1, K3, P14, K3, P1. Rep. these 2 rows for 11 ridges of garter-st, ending on wrong side.

TURN HEEL:
Row 1:sl 1, K10, SKP(sl 1, K1, pass slipped st.over), K1, turn.
Row 2:sl 1, P2, P2tog, P1, turn.   Row 3:sl 1, K3, SKP,K1, turn.
Row 4:sl 1, P4, P2tog, P1, turn.   Row 5:sl 1, K5, SKP,K1, turn.
Row 6:sl 1, P6, P2tog, P1, turn.   Row 7:sl 1, K7, SKP,K1, turn.
Row 8:sl 1, P8, P2tog, P1, turn.   Row 9:sl 1, K9, SKP,P1, turn.
Row10:sl 1, P10,P2tog, turn. Cut nylon.

SHAPE GUSSETS:
Rnd.1:1st needle:(heel)sl 1, K11, pick up 13sts. along heel flap.
      2nd needle:Work the 22 sts. of instep.
      3rd needle:Pick up 13 sts. along heel, K6 from 1st needle.
Rnd.2:1st needle:K to within last 2 sts, K 2 tog.   (60 sts)
      2nd needle:Work even.
      3rd needle:SKP, K to end.
Rnd.3:Work even. Rep rnds 2 and 3 until 44 sts. remain. Work even until foot measures 2½" less than desired. Join in nylon.

SHAPE TOE:
Rnd.1:1st needle:K to within last 4 sts, K2tog, K2.
      2nd needle:K2, SKP, K to within last 4 sts, K2tog, K2.
      3rd needle:K2, SKP, K to end.
Rnd.2:Work even. Rep rnds.1 and 2 until 20 sts remain.
Break yarn and weave toe together, using Kitchener stitch.

MOCK-STOCKS or DE-FEETS.
Same GAUGE, same number of sts; less wool, less work. Why bother with feet? They make your brain creak, need much washing, and wear out first. They take up room in ski-boots. So stop at the ankle. For the last 10 rnds, inc 2 sts at each side every 2nd rnd, which will cause your mock--stock to dip nicely at the ankles. End with 4 ridges of garter-st. UNNECESSARY ON RIBBING Attach wide elastic to go under foot. For apres-ski, knit a little tab to cover the instep.

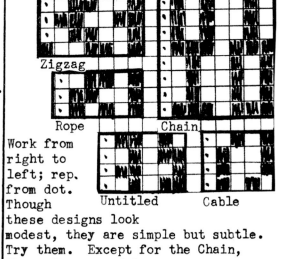

Zigzag

Rope   Chain

Untitled   Cable

Work from right to left; rep. from dot. Though these designs look modest, they are simple but subtle. Try them. Except for the Chain, there is no need to carry your yarn more than 2 sts, and they make handsome vertical patterns.

"Busy Knitter"(me). This 10-week television series is now handled by ETS. Starting dates as follows:-
Feb.19, WHRO Norfolk, Va., April 2, WMSB E. Lansing, Mich., April 9, KLRM Austin and San Antonio,Tex.,
April 23, WTVS Detroit, Mich., May 21, WGBU Bowling Green, Ohio. Watch your local program guides to
see if it is coming to your area, and if not, suggest it to your station. (Study Guides now $1.50.)

So this letter will go to some new people, including Peggy Chester's "Popular Needlework" readers.
I had better explain my knitting viewpoint. I am sworn to making knitting pleasant,and to abolishing
unpopular things such as purling, sewing-up, and, when practicable, casting off. Thus I have evolved
my own knitting method, and embody this in my semi-annual newsletters. I prefer natural unbleached
wool. Having found sources for this, I am glad to retail it to those who share my tastes. To my mind
knitting can be a craft, and I have been fortunate in being accepted by craft exhibits. So consider
using my yarns. Take my designs as a starting-point only, and turn out your own works of art.

Now I am learning to spin, and find Icelandic wool perfect for such a beginner as I am. It is all
pulled out and ready to spin, and I can use 1, 2, or 3 thickness together. Marion L. Channing has
published a fine new book, "The Magic of Spinning". It costs $1.65 ppd.from handspinner and black-
-sheep-raiser Paula Simmons, Suquamish, Washington 98392.

Another splendid book to be strongly recommended is "101 Ways to Improve Your Knitting" by Barbara
Abbey. It is full of hints and salty admonitions, and I can send you a copy for $1 ppd.

Happy Knitting, then, and have a happy summer, stocking up on stockings.

Elizabeth writes:

I believe that M-squared over something equals X because I consider Einstein a sapient man and others whom I consider clever endorse this. It wouldn't do me any good to disbelieve it, as I have no way of proving the contrary.

*For years I had a wonderful time believing in the Piltdown man. I also believed that spinach was the most nourishing vegetable, that if you ate an orange and then drank a glass of milk you might as well reserve a room at the hospital, that modesty is a desirable attribute, that books must be hoarded and never thrown away no matter how meretricious, that a dog is he and a cat she, that **everybody** has to get out into the lovely fresh open air every day or go into a decline, that you have to wait two hours after a meal before going swimming for goodness sake, that roast beef makes you strong as a bull, that riding back to the engine makes you throw up, that if you hold a guinea-pig up by its tail its eyes fall out – I could go on and on.*

These charmingly archaic beliefs did me – perhaps – no harm, but they certainly cluttered up my head; I could have disproved every one of them if I'd given my mind to it.

I now put what I consider important matters to the best test I can find, which often regrettably boils down to my instinct and common sense. After over sixty years this turns out to be a reliable touchstone; it's all I have, anyway.

I truly believe I know the best way for me personally to knit. I truly believe this to be the most beautiful summer in human memory. I truly believe what I have just discovered: that field-campions, after sunset, smell just like carnations. As to the question of collecting schoolhouses, I truly believe it to be a manifestation of amiable lunacy, but it is our lunacy and harms no one. (continued on page 118)

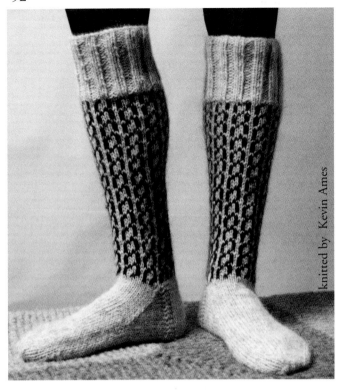

knitted by Kevin Ames

knitted by Jackie Ritchie

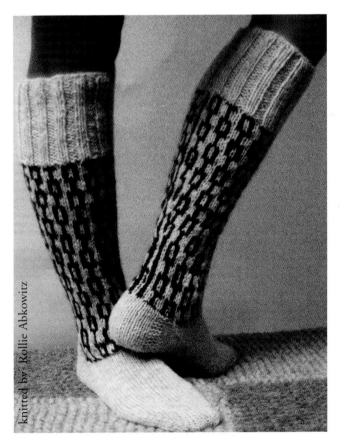

knitted by Rollie Abkowitz

knitted by Dale Long

Elizabeth Zimmermann

Sweater knitted by Jinny Lee Waters & Diane Zangl. Stockings knitted by Dale Long

T h e   O p i n i o n a t e d   K n i t t e r

Elizabeth Zimmermann LTD.

ELIZABETH ZIMMERMANN
BOX 5555 MILWAUKEE, WIS. 53211

Newsletter and leaflet #19
SPIRAL HAT; BOOKS   Fall '67
Free until spring '68; then 25¢

Dear Knitter,

The best part of Christmas is present-planning. Try some Spiral Hats. They are inter-
-esting to make and inexpensive. Knit one in an evening. It is very like my "pixie hat" in Woman's
Day, but directions are simpler. The largest available 16" circular needle is #10½, so knit loosely.

SPIRAL HAT. GAUGE: 7½ sts. to 3". MATERIALS: 1 skein Sheepsdown, 1 16" circular needle #10½, 1 set of
sock-needles #10½. (If hard to find, sharpen single-pointed needles in the pencil-sharpener...)
CAST ON 50 sts. on circular needle. K 5 rows back and forth. Next row (right
side) K2, M1(by making backwa rd loop over R needle) around. (75 sts). Join.
Now pay careful attention, as you will repeat the following for 20 rnds:-
P2, P2 tog, K 11, M1. Rep. from, and keep repeating. Pattern will edge to
the left. Remember the M1, and count sts carefully until pattern is estab-
-lished. At 20 rnds, eliminate the M1, and hat starts coming to a point.
at 35 sts. change to 4 needles. At 20 sts. start slipping the remaining K st, knitting the next, and
psso. At 5 sts. fasten off. Sew border, and steam in a spiral. You can squeeze two of these out of
one skein of Sheepsdown. The model was designed for this yarn, and there is no "just as good". This
sounds commercial, but is true. For a larger cap, work 25 rnds. before starting to decrease.

RARE KNITTING BOOKS. Why thumb hopelessly through the glossy, floppy "Books" for exactly the sweater
you want? Start your own hard-cover knitting library, and yourself design what you have in mind.
Many of the following are unobtainable in the US, so you see that I am continuing with my policy of
selling only what is hard to find. I have included some embroidery books too. Sorry about the price-
-increase; I had been carrying books as an accomodation, and my accountant says I must be realistic,
(horrid word). BUT you may subtract 50¢ each for the second and all subsequent books in one order.

MARY THOMAS'S KNITTING BOOK. $5.50 ppd. The tried
and true. Detailed illustrated directions for all
knitting techniques. Socks, gloves, mittens, etc.

MARY THOMAS'S BOOK OF KNITTING PATTERNS. $5.50 ppd
Just what it says; hundreds of stitch-patterns in
plain, textured, and lace knitting.

MARY THOMAS'S EMBROIDERY BOOK. $5.50 ppd. Basic
manual of 30 different kinds of embroidery.

MARY THOMAS'S DICTIONARY OF EMBROIDERY STITCHES.
$5.50 ppd. 305 distinct stitches, all illustrated.

ENCYCLOPEDIA OF NEEDLEWORK. $5.50 ppd. English
edition of Thérèse de Dillmont's 1886 classic. 788
pp; 1174 engravings. Knitting, crochet, embroidery
of all kinds, tatting, macramé, lace, needlepoint.

TRADITIONAL KNITTING PATTERNS. $10.50 ppd.By James
Norbury, English TV knitter. Directions for, and
photographs of, 263 European pattern-stitches.

FIRST BOOK OF MODERN LACE KNITTING. $6.00 ppd. By
Marianne Kinzel,Austrian designer. Lovely designs
adaptable to stoles, elegant lacy afghans, heir-
-loom Christening shawls, or shawls for Grandma.

SECOND BOOK OF MODERN LACE KNITTING. $6.00 ppd
Companion to the above. Both are out of print,
but I still have a modest stock.

NORWEGIAN KNITTING DESIGNS. $4.50 ppd. By Annchen
Sibbern-Bøhn. A very Scandinavian book (in Engl-
-ish) with graphs for typical mittens and ski-
-stockings, and two lovely traditional sweaters.

CROSS-STITCH PATTERNS. $4.30 ppd. By Heinz-Edgar
Kiewe, tapestry, knitting, and embroidery author-
-ity in Oxford. Very useful for colour-pattern
designs in knitting.

101 WAYS TO IMPROVE YOUR KNITTING.$1.50 paperback.
By Barbara Abbey, knitting artist at Pell Lake,
Wis. Down-to-earth information and advice.

"GUERNSEY AND JERSEY KNITTING PATTERNS" by Gladys Thompson. The new edition still hangs fire, so I shall start a 1-book Lending Library with my treasured extra copy. For #1 you may keep it two weeks; third and every subsequent week costs $50, OK? So hurry and get on the waiting-list. I know this is putting the Honour System to the test, but, as Martha Chace says, "All knitters splendid people."

"THE BUSY KNITTER" TV SERIES (me) starts on the following stations, the weeks beginning:-

| Aug 20th. KAET,Tempe,Ariz. | Sept 3rd. WUFT,Gainesville,Fla. | Oct 1st. WGTE,Toledo,Ohio. |
| Aug 20th. KCSD,Kansas City,Mo. | Sept 10th.WUCM,University City,Mich. | Nov 12th.WTTW,Chicago,Ill. |

That makes about 25 runnings of this 10-week knitting series, many owing to your having created a demand. Thank you. If you would like to see it in your area, pester your ETV Station Manager. Tell him it is now handled by ETS, 317 E. Second St., Bloomington, Indiana. 47401

CUSTOM-SPUN AND -WOVEN TWEED, no less. Paula Simmons will handspin, and Lester Mayhew handweave, a skirtlength to match your Icelandic sweater. $30 for an average skirt, straight or A-line, with gener--ous hem. (1 2/3 yds, 32"-35" wide. 50¢ an inch, if you want more, or less.) Order from me, at the same time as the yarn, and I will send sufficient wool to Paula.

ALAS, everything is going up, even postage, and my prices will too. Expect a price-increase about the first of the year. But my yarns are so economical in use that it's not so bad as it sounds.

Oh yes; study the sweaters on pp 46 and 47 of McCall's Fall-Winter '67-'68 (not the one with the fancy sleeves), and on pp 36 and 11 of Woman's Day Knitting Book #5 (not the white cable job). They are all by our daughter Meg Swansen or by me.

sincerely Elizabeth.

#18.   All rights reserved.
If you wish to quote, ask me.

Elizabeth also referred to this design as a conch, snail, or Dairy Queen hat.

Instructions for this 3-spiral version are on the following page.

Snail hat and 3 + 1 Sweater (NL#13, page 74) knitted by Meg Swansen Carol Anderson knitted the Tomten Jacket (NL#7, page 44)

Several years after Newsletter #19 was printed, Elizabeth re-designed the Snail Hat to have three spirals instead of five – and, more significantly, she maintained the sharp fold along the garter-stitch strip all the way to the bitter end by continuing the Make 1 increase and adding another decrease to shape the top.

You will probably need more than the recommended one skein of Sheepsdown now, unless you shorten the hat; see the notes on page 53.

Three-Spiral Hat
(as opposed to the Five-Spiral in the NL)

Gauge and needle as above.
Cast On 40.

Knit back and forth for 5 rows (2-1/2 ridges).
Increase 50% (to 60 stitches) by working K2, Make 1 across.
Join and work around as follows:
*P2, P2tog, K16, M1.
Repeat from * around for 18 rounds.
Shape top as follows:
(P1, P2tog twice, K15, M1) 3 times.
Continue around and note that each round will have 3 fewer stitches and the plain knit-sections will start to narrow while still spiralling.
Continue until you have 15 stitches. For the last round, (P2tog twice, K1, M1) 3 times. Run wool through the final 12 stitches and finish off.

above: Meg holding young Liesl who is wearing tights (page 88) knitted by Elizabeth. Photographer, Chris, is reflected on the left.

left: Liesl holding young Renata who is wearing the Baby Surprise jacket. Photographer, Meg, is reflected on the left ... an unconscious reenactment.

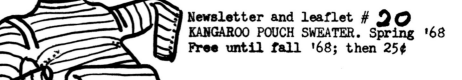

Elizabeth Zimmermann LTD.

E L I Z A B E T H   Z I M M E R M A N N
BOX 5555 MILWAUKEE, WIS. 53211

Newsletter and leaflet # 20
KANGAROO POUCH SWEATER. Spring '68
Free until fall '68; then 25¢

Dear Knitter,
    The name "Kangaroo Sweater" comes from its pouchlike construction, not its finished appearance, which is of a classic sweater with perfectly-inserted, well-fitting sleeves. It is an adventure, designed for those dedicated to circular knitting, and simpler than it seems. Sleeves are picked up and worked down; sleeve-caps are shaped like sock-heels. It has side-darts, & subtle shaping at lower back. Make it in stocking-st with horizontal stripes of colour or of purling.

MATERIALS for average size; 40" around, 25" long, with long sleeves:-
4 skeins "Homespun"........5 sts. to 1"   3 wheels 1-ply Icelandic wool..5 or 6 sts. to 1"
5 skeins 2-ply Sheepswool..5 sts. to 1"   5 wheels 2-ply Icelandic wool..4 sts. to 1"
6 skeins Fisherman Yarn....5 or 4½ sts. to 1"   7 skeins 4-ply Sheepswool......3 sts. to 1"
7 skeins 3-ply Sheepswool..4 sts. to 1"   7 skeins Sheepsdown............3 or 2½ sts. to 1"
1 24" and 1 16" circular needle, of a size between #5 and #10½, to give you the above GAUGES.

GAUGE: Make a swatch 30 sts. wide and about 4" long, take it off the needle, steam it gently, measure how many sts. there are to 3". Divide by 3 to find average number of sts. per inch. The result is your GAUGE. Multiply your GAUGE by number of inches needed around bust. This is the number of sts. you will need. The sweater below is 40" around; 200 sts. at a GAUGE of 5 sts. to 1". If you have more sts., or less, use the percentages given as your guide in shaping.

BODY: With 24" needle cast on 190sts.(5% less than 200) Join, being careful not to twist. K around for 3". Inc. 10sts. evenly spaced across back only. (200 sts.) At 13" make BUST DARTS: Starting at R u.arm, turn, P100, turn, K98, turn, P96, turn, K94, and so on until you have P72, always slipping 1st. st. Continue around. At holes made by turns pick up st. under st. on R needle, put it on L needle and K2tog. At 15" or desired length to u.arm make KANGAROO POUCH: *Put 20sts.(10% of 200) on thread at R u.arm. Cast on 2 by making 2 backward loops over R needle. Work to L u.arm and rep from*. Continue around for 7"(classic depth for most armholes). Cast off 82sts. for front. Work back and forth on back, casting off 3 sts. at beg. of each row until 46sts. remain(23% of 200!)Place these on thread. Mark armholes by basting down between 2 cast-on sts. on each side. Machine-st. twice each side

SLEEVE: With 16" needle pick up 20 sts. at u.arm and 2sts. for every 3 rows around armhole.(65-70sts.) Work around for 1".
SLEEVECAP: Work to 5sts. past shoulder--seam, sl 1, K 1, psso, turn.
sl 1, P 10, P 2 tog, P 1, turn.
sl 1, K 11, sl 1, K 1, psso, turn.
sl 1, P 12, P 2 tog, P 1, turn.
sl 1, K 13, sl 1, K 1, psso, turn. Continue thus, decreasing by working tog. the 2 sts. each side of gap, and working 1 more st. before turning. When sts. on needle total 66(33% of 200), work straight to elbow, about 7". Now decr. 2sts. at u.arm (K2 tog, K1, sl 1, K1, psso) every 5th rnd. until 50 sts.(25% of 200) remain for 3/4 sleeve, or 40sts(20% of 200)for long sleeve. Try on for correct sleeve-length. P 1 rnd. Change to thinner yarn if you have it. Work 1" for hem. (If hem is same yarn, decr 10%) Don't cast off but sew down loose--ly. Pick up around neck and work CREW NECK as wished. P1 rnd and work hem in same yarn.

of basting with small st. and loose tension. Cut
on basting. Sew shoulders.Pick up sts around low-
-er edge,P1 rnd,decr 10%. Work hem, for 2".

TURTLE NECK:Work in K2,P2 ribbing until you are
sick of it. Cast off loosely in ribbing.

SLEEVELESS SHELL: Pick up around armhole at the rate of 1st. in every 2nd row. P 1 rnd, make hem.
DRESS: Simply start sooner, according to taste, on 200 sts. Eliminate lower back shaping.

NOTES AND COMMENT.
"Busy Knitter" (me), 10-week television series, is showing now at KDPS Des Moines,Ia., KERA Dallas,
Texas, KTWV Topeka,Ka.,WCNY Liverpool,N.Y., WBRA Roanoke,Va. Watch your schedule, and create demand
at your station. There will be a second series next fall, in colour. Busy Knitter RIDES AGAIN!

Sweater #2504 on p.7 of Pauline Denham book #25 is mine, also centre one in Spinnerin book #180 p.21.
This one was knitted by Meg, and resembles my prize-winning French sweater which was accepted last
fall for the Wisconsin Designer-Craftsmen's Annual Exhibit.I think you will enjoy the shaded leaves.

BOOK NEWS: Admirers of Gladys Thompson, take heart; the publishers again promise her new book for
next fall. In the meantime I can recommend, and supply, two excellent French books (floppy); the
new "Tricots Enfants" in French, put out by Jardin des Modes in Parie, and an English translation
of their "Grammaire de Tricot", called "Handbook for Better Knitting", which contains many fine
French finishing touches. $1 each. I also have the Scotch Wool Shop Knitting Book, now 25 years
old, with directions for many classic and traditional garments for children and adults. 60¢.
Postage and handling 50¢ on any or all of the above.

Bottom of the page already. Good Knitting; keep your eyes open.

As for the instruction to increase 5% across the back only: this was a concession to fashion back in 1968. Remember the slouch-model look?: hips forward, one foot pointed out at an angle, shoulders sloped, back curved. If you increase as instructed, the back will blouse slightly to help create that image. To eliminate the blousing, increase all in one round above a ribbing -- or increase one stitch each side of two or three side "seam" stitches, every few inches.

Bust Dart instruction: we now use Barbara G. Walker's method (first revealed in *Knitting From the Top*) for invisible short-rows-and-wrapping as follows:

Starting at R u.arm, slip next stitch to R needle (purl-wise), bring wool to front (between the needles), replace slipped stitch to L needle, turn. See how the working wool is wrapped around the slipped stitch? Purl 100. Slip next stitch to R needle. Take wool to other side (between the needles), replace slipped stitch to L needle. Turn. K 98. Continue as written, except - instead of slipping each first stitch, work the "wrap" as just described.

After the short rows are done and you prepare to work the next complete round: when you come to a wrap, put the tip of the R needle under the wrap and into the slipped stitch and knit the two strands together.

Keep the wrap quite loose -- especially when working it on the purl side. You can easily snug up a too-loose wrap, but a too-tight wrap will dimple the fabric and it is more difficult to loosen.

Another option: after the first wrap, instead of turning your work, try Knittting Back Backwards instead. Continue to work forward and backward and wrap at each turn. When you knit the wraps and slipped stitches together, the turning points will melt into the fabric.

knitted by Judy Franklin

Elizabeth Zimmermann

The Opinionated Knitter

Elizabeth Zimmermann LTD.

ELIZABETH ZIMMERMANN
BOX 5555   MILWAUKEE, WIS. 53211

Newsletter and leaflet # **21**
SURPRISE JACKET. Fall '68
Free until spring '69; then 25¢

Dear Knitter,
        I call it the "Surprise Jacket" because it looks like nothing on earth when you have
finished knitting it. Sew up two seams, and you find you have the nicest little garter-stitch baby-
-sweater you could wish to see, reversible, and with no side or armhole seams to look ill-fitting or
feel uncomfortable. And there is no breaking-off or joining-in of yarn. Made in baby wool, at 6 sts.
to 1", it is a fine present for the new-born, and will "grow" with the baby. Same directions and
Fisherman Yarn, or 2-ply Sheepswool, at 5 sts. to 1", give the right size for a 1-year-old, or older.

SURPRISE JACKET. Materials: 3oz. baby wool(GAUGE 6 sts. to 1")or 2 skeins Fisherman Yarn(GAUGE 5 sts.
to 1"). 1 pr. needles to give you either of these GAUGES. Five very pretty little buttons.
Make a SWATCH to determine GAUGE, and CAST ON 160 sts. With safety-pins mark 36th and 125th sts.

1. K34,sl 1,K2 tog,psso,K86,sl 1,K2 tog,psso,K34.
2 and all even-numbered rows, Knit.
3. K33,sl 1,K2 tog,psso,K84,sl 1,K2 tog,psso,K33.
5. K32,sl 1,K2 tog,psso,K82,sl 1,K2 tog,psso,K32.
7. K31,sl 1,K2 tog,psso,K80,sl 1,K2 tog,psso,K31,

> psso = pass slipped stitch over.
> 1 ridge = 2 rows.
> M1 = Make one by backward loop over R needle.

See what you are doing? You are decreas-
-ing 2 at each marked st, making 2
diagonal lines, and 2 corners. At
5 ridges inc. 9 sts(K3,M1) across
end sections, believe it or not
for fullness above CUFF. After
22 decr. (90sts), work 3 rows
even, then start to inc. at same
points, by M1 each side of mark-
-ed st. every 2nd row. Work will
start to look v. odd, indeed,
but trust me, and press on. At
114 sts, inc.10sts in 1 row
evenly-spaced across centre
section for BACK FULLNESS. At
152 sts, shape NECK by casting off
5 sts. at beg. of next two rows. When
there are 158sts, work on centre 90sts.
only, for 10 ridges, Hope you are still
with me. Now pick up 10 sts. from side of
piece just knitted, K 34sts. from end of needle.
Work next row, repeating this process(178sts). Mark 44th and 135th sts, and start increasing by M1
each side of marked st every 2nd row. After 3 ridges, work 5 small buttonholes(yarn over K2tog)
evenly-spaced on end-sections. Work 3 ridges and cast off, fairly loosely, in purl, on right side.
Funny-looking object, isn't it? Well, study the drawing, match A to A and B to B, join with a neat
woven seam, and hey presto eureka and lo -- a baby-sweater! When you know if it's a boy or girl,
sew buttons over buttonholes on appropriate side. The baby will probably be unmoved by this offer-
-ing, but the mother may well be charmed, and your friends will be AMAZED.

What else is new? WMVS-TV in Milwaukee has made me into a second television knitting series. "Busy
Knitter 2" consists of 13 half-hours, in colour, dealing with colour-pattern knitting, as shewn in
the making of a ski-sweater. (7 skeins 3-ply Sheepswool, 5 light, 2 dark. Adv.) The series is avail-
-able from ETS, 371 E. 2nd St., Bloomington, Ind., 47401, so pressure your local ETV stations to run

it. "Busy Knitter 1" still going strong; here are stations and dates at time of going to press:-

KTEH, San Jose, Cal	starts Aug 18	WSJK, Binghampton, N.Y.	starts Sept 29th
Alabama ETV, Auburn,Ala.	" Sept 8	WTVS, Detroit, Mich.	" Sept 29th
WTTW, Chicago, Ill.	" Sept 22	WGBH, Boston, Mass	" Dec 1st

Watch your local papers for dates of "Busy Knitter 2", which is not yet scheduled, but I think Boston plans to run it after the re-run of "Busy Knitter 1".

Then I have a new book,"Step-by-Step Knitting" by Mary Walker Phillips. $1.95 + 50¢ postage and handling; postfree if ordered with other books. It shews how to knit many beautiful and useful things other than sweaters, and includes excellent instructions for the poor things who knit back- -wards with their left hands. But don't forget, if you are left-handed and starting to knit, learn the "German" way, with yarn over L forefinger. This is easier for you than for the right-handed.

The best news is that I am about to join the happy gang of doating grandmas,(hence the above design). From now on you may expect more baby designs from me, gradually increasing in age and size. X I have deliberately held off until I had a personal interest in this field, and results may well be surpris- -ing, to say the least. Have you realized how unbecoming pink and blue are to a bran-new baby? But white is always successful, and how about silver-grey or medium brown with touches of white? Deeper shades suit the baby, whether brown- or blue-eyed, and will stay fresh-looking, which will delight the young mother. I am laying in a small stock of real Shetland wool from the Shetland Isles in White, Silver, Beige, medium Brown, and Lovat, all heather tones, the last one being an indescrib- -able soft green, the colour of the Scottish hills on a misty day. This wool is beautifully soft, knits up at 6 sts to 1", and costs $1.60 for 2 oz. Wonderful for shawls.

Well, I think that will do for this time. Knit, and keep calm.

Sincerely Elizabeth.

#21   All rights reserved.   X *my husband says, like me.* If you wish to quote, ask me.

Consider:
- I-Cord Cast Off, or an Applied I-Cord trim around all the edges, either a single application, or multiple layers.
- If the jacket is made with wool heavier than Shetland, a hood is a handsome addition; see the Tomten Hood. page 42
- Before you sew up the shoulders, have some fun by tossing it to someone (knitter or not) and challenge them to fold that amorphous bit of knitting into a sweater.
- After-Thought-Pockets may be added to the lower, horizontal section; see page 114.
- Since my mother's initial, hesitant importing of a few shades of Shetland wool, we have now expanded to stocking all 160 colors of that lovely stuff.

Nancie Kremer writes, "The other way I add sleeve-length is to Cast On 36 sts, do a rib cuff, increase 9 sts, then work as many additional rows of garter stitch as I need for extra length. I do both cuffs/ sleeves this way then cast on the 92 sts that go between the sleeves and continue the pattern as written."

More comments from happy BSJ knitters:
"I'm on my sixth *Baby Surprise Sweater* in four months and wonder: is there some way to stop...?"

"I figure I have made at least 45 of these sweaters."

"I am filled with admiration and respect for the genius that went into this creation."

"I've been knitting them *(Baby Surprise Jackets)* over and over and over for the past five or six years; I love them! You have to admit this is by far the most adorable baby sweater ever!"

"I enjoy knitting this little sweater as it is truly fun. I've made more than 50 in the last 3 years."!

"This sweater is an engineering marvel."

"I've been making little people sweaters for at least 40 years and haven't found an easier pattern yet; LOVE the BSJ..."

"I did not think it possible to have more respect for your mother than I already had. Well...never say never. To design such an incredible sweater staggers my imagination. She was truly an engineering genius!"

knitted by Meg Swansen
Footed Longies knitted by Jean Krebs (NL#17, page 88)

Elizabeth's Baby Surprise Jacket has taken on almost legendary status since it was first designed in 1968. Its inception, as accurately as I have been able to determine, is as follows: Elizabeth and Gaffer had taken a trip home to Europe and in Germany (with her first grandchild due to be born that November), Elizabeth had picked up a pattern for a typical garter-stitch baby bonnet which, by means of double-decreasing, came to a peak in the middle of the forehead. A few inches into the project she lost the instructions and, after fussing with it for a while, tossed it aside.

When she went to retrieve it the following morning, the

Elizabeth Zimmermann

Hat (NL#22) and hooded BSJ
Jacket knitted by Meg Swansen
Baby Longies knitted by Jean
Krebs (NL#17)

configuration in which it lay looked as if it might be the sleeve of a baby jacket. With that image in mind, Elizabeth continued knitting.

After the first few models, she modified the design to include narrower cuffs and increases across the back to accommodate diapers.

It was an immediate success and Elizabeth found herself pressured to come up with an Adult version. She resisted because the proportions of this jacket produce a relatively short sleeve, and she didn't like the appearance of obvious Knitting-Up to lengthen them. Check page 112 - 114 to see how this was resolved.

Also, there is now an Adult-Baby Surprise Jacket; see pages 106 - 107.

knitted by Meg Swansen

The popularity of Elizabeth's 1968 design continues to present day and there is a chat room devoted to helping knitters produce this jacket (*http://babysurprise0.tripod.com*). The list was instigated by two generous knitters, Gail Bable and Mary Bastian. One of Gail's students, Kim Hershfeldt, wanted to enlarge the pattern, so chose very thick wool and a size 13 needle; the resulting jacket fits an adult.

As soon as I read that on the list, I rushed to my needles and, using 4-ply Unspun Icelandic wool, on #10-1/2 needles, at about 2-1/2 sts to an inch, I followed the Baby Surprise instructions –- with the same baby-number of stitches – and produced the sweater you see here; an Adult Baby Jacket. It continues to surprise.

Knit a few baby versions first, to give you a grasp of the concept. My modifications include Carol Anderson's idea to cast on invisibly (178 stitches instead of 160 as I eliminated the 18-stitch fullness above the cuffs); add a few vertical inches at center back to lengthen the body, and eliminate the increase across the back waist. From the raw sleeve stitches, I worked 5-6" of additional length, then decreased severely for long, snug cuffs, ending with Elizabeth's I-Cord Cast Off in a contrasting color. For a continuous stream of I-Cord, using Joyce Williams' variation of EZ's Applied I-Cord (*see page 55)*, the seam is united up the cuff/sleeve (picking up stitches from the selvedges and working 3-Needle I-Cord Cast Off), continued across the neck-back, "seamed" down the other sleeve and ended with EZ's I-Cord Casting Off around the second cuff. Then I worked a bead of EZ's Applied I-Cord from one shoulder, around the neck front, down one side, around the lower edge and up the other side to the second shoulder; add extra I-Cord roundlettes at each corner to turn 90-degrees. Weave end to shoulder seam.

E l i z a b e t h   Z i m m e r m a n n

The Opinionated Knitter

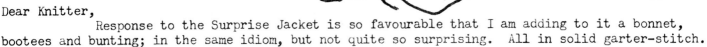

Elizabeth Zimmermann LTD.

ELIZABETH ZIMMERMANN
BOX 5555   MILWAUKEE, WIS. 53211

Newsletter and leaflet #22
BONNET, BOOTEES, BUNTING.
Spring 1969
Free until fall '69; then 25¢

Dear Knitter,

        Response to the Surprise Jacket is so favourable that I am adding to it a bonnet, bootees and bunting; in the same idiom, but not quite so surprising. All in solid garter-stitch.

BONNET. Size: 3 months and up.
GAUGE: 6 sts. to 1". MATERIALS:
2oz. Shetland wool, 1 pr. suitable
needles. Cast on 122 sts.
Row 1. K24,SK2P,K68,SK2P,K24.
Row 2. and all alternate rows,K.
Row 3. K23,SK2P,K66,SK2P,K23.
Row 5. K22,SK2P,K64,SK2P,K22.
Continue thus, keeping decreases in line. On
row 11,K5,M1, across(122 sts.). When ends are
decreased away(26 sts.),..knit up 1 st. on each
ridge along end-pieces(84 sts). *Next row, decr.
7 sts. evenly spaced across(K10,K2tog.). K 1 row.
Rep. from* until 7 sts remain. Finish off and
sew up back. Sew on button and make loop. For
HOOD: K up 50 sts on lower edge.*K8,inc.7 evenly
spaced across(M1,K6). K 1 row. Rep. from* until
you have 100 sts. Work 4 ridges and cast off.

BOOTEES. Size: small. GAUGE: 6 sts. to 1" approx.
MATERIALS: Oddments of any fine yarn,1 pair
suitable needles. Cast on 51 stitches.
Row 1. K11,SK2P,K23,SK2P,K11.
Row 2 and all alternate rows,K.
Row 3. K10,SK2P,K21,SK2P,K10.
Row 5. K9, SK2P,K19,SK2P,K9.
Continue thus,keeping decreases in
line until ends are used up(3 sts.)
off each end-piece(27 sts.). Knit up 12 sts.
Row 1. K12,M1,K1,M1,K1,M1,K1,M1,K12.
Row 2 and all alternate rows,Knit.
Row 3. K13,M1,K1,M1,K3,M1,K1,M1,K13.
Row 5. K14,M1,K1,M1,K5,M1,K1,M1,K14.
Continue thus until you have 51 sts. Work 4 ridges
even. Next row,K2tog.3 times,K14,K2tog.6 times,K13,
K2tog.3 times. K to centre, weave sides tog,sew up
back. Make 14" tie and attach at back of ankle.

BUNTING. Size:36"X 18" approx. GAUGE: 2½sts. to 1". MATERIALS: 7-8 skeins Sheepsdown.
1 pr lg. needles (#10½-#15). Cast on 40 sts. by invisible cast-on method in Mary Thomas
p.66. *K39,turn,K back. K38,turn,K back. K37,turn,K back, and so on until you have
K5,turn,K back. NOW: K6,turn,K back. K7,turn,K back, and so on, taking up one more
waiting st. every 2nd row until you have 40 again. Rep from* 3 times. Weave end to
beginning. You have a square. *K up 1 st.for each ridge along one side. Work 4 ridges
Cast off. Rep.from* on all sides. On 4th side cast off 16 sts.on each end, and work
12 ridges on centre 40 sts. Then work back and forth on centre 10 sts, knitting 2 tog
at end of each row, to consume gradually the end-pieces. When consumed, cast off.
This forms a good headcover.X Fold sides to middle, sew up bottom, and insert strong
zipper in front. For a small baby the lower 1/3 can be folded up over feet, keeping
them warm and snug; you can even put in the baby plus his clip-board. For next winter
take it apart, unravel hood, and you have what may easily become a beloved Linus-blanket.

X SEW CORNERS

USEFUL NOTES ON ABOVE. SK2P = sl 1, K2tog,pass sl.st.over. M1 = Make 1 by putting backward loop over
R needle. To weave garter-st, see leaflet #7. You may slip all first sts if you wish; I do.
I never give needle-sizes, as people knit so differently in the matter of tightness or looseness.

Elizabeth writes: I carry on a running and experimental battle with the making of black bread. Sometimes it's better than others, but it's always edible. We never did accustom ourselves to grocery bread, though I must admit we didn't try very hard. It would take childhood indoctrination to learn to tolerate anything so bland, rubbery, tasteless and eternally fresh. Do you know why French bread is so famous for its excellence? They bake it three times a day and you buy it three times a day; its freshness is genuine.

BUSY KNITTER 2 is launched. Ski-sweater; colour; 13 weeks; guest-star, the cat KLINE. If you want to make the identical sweater, use 3-ply Sheepswool,4-5 Cream,2-3 Oatmeal. Here are places & dates:

| KTCA St Paul | Feb 2 | WGBH Boston Feb 16 | WETA Washington DC March 9 | WVIZ Cleveland O March 23 |
| WMHT Schenectady | Feb 16 | WHA Madison March 2 | KAET Tempe,Ariz March 23 | |

Busy Knitter 1 now running on KQED San Francisco, and perhaps other stations. Available from ETS, 512 E 17,POBox 1430, Bloomington, Ind 47401. Mail is always effective, so ask your station to run it.

WONDERFUL NEW BOOK ; $10, and worth thribble the money. "Treasury of Knitting Patterns" by Barbara Walker contains well over 500 knitting stitches, excellently described, and illustrated by clear photographs. Mrs Walker writes as one human being communicating with another; remarkable, to say the least, in knitting books. I also have "America's Knitting Book"($10) by Gertrude Taylor.
Is your "101 Ways" wearing out? I have a hard-cover edition for $2. Add 50¢ per order on all book orders, for postage and handling. (Hush! I believe that Gladys Thompson is c o m i n g   c l o s e r)

SHETLAND WOOL in beguiling dark heather shades will be available in the fall. I already have Silver, Beige,White, Brown, and Blue Lovat. Let me know if you would like samples when they are ready.

MEG SWANSEN (Knitting Workshop, 160 S.Main,New Hope, Pa 18938. Tel:215-862-2142) now confines herself to mailorder and "by appointment only". She carries all my yarns, so Eastern knitters may save time by ordering from her. (Also splendid wool braid from Norway. Samples $1, refunded on first $5 order)

SHIRLEY GRADE in Elm Grove,Wis.has my yarns available; also help! Telephone her for times;786-6346.

I have a sweater in "Fabrics and Fibres" exhibit at the John Michael Kohler Art Center in Sheboygan through March 24. Also a "Hanging"(bring your smelling-salts) in the annual Wisconsin Designer Craftsmen Exhibit at Villa Terrace in Milwaukee, March 23 - April 20.
Sweaters on p.11 of McCall's Knitting Book #4 are mine, also bonnets in the back of Feb Woman's Day.

NOW, let us all take a deep breath, and forge on into the future; knitting at the ready.

Sincerely Elizabeth

German bread is quite different but just as good. Why does the Anglo-Saxon scorn black bread? It is mentioned with nose wrinkled and as a child I was frightened by the very words. I thought of bread the color, texture and taste of coal. When the reader-aloud came to the part where the poor charcoal burner's children had nothing to eat but black bread, my eyes would fill with tears as they did for the little match-girl.

When I first tasted black bread on its native heath, my mind changed fast; black bread was delicious.

Now when I stand beneath my rapidly-growing white pines and listen for the wind in their tops, I close my eyes and am transported back to Spring skiing in the German Alps. The South slopes would be already almost snowless and the whole hillside dripping, trickling and running with the melt of higher snows, hurrying to the valley. There we would sit at noon, sleeves rolled up, noses lanolined, our jaws chomping rhythmically on black bread and Landjaeger. Lulled by lunch and by the plop and tinkle of running water, we often took a nap until woken by the coolness of the shadows in late afternoon. Then we would plod up the mountain if it was Saturday -- or whoop down into the valley if it was Sunday; the weekend over and the city beckoning.

That was all a long time ago, but the scent and sound of pines stays with me and triggers the memory of black bread.

Baby Surprise Jacket: NL#21, p 102
Pink bonnet: NL#22, page 108
Fair Isle yoke sweater: page 8; all
knitted by Meg Swansen.
Blue Ski Bonnet: NL#11, page 60
knitted by Renate Baur

above: Elizabeth's granddaughter, Liesl, wearing the Hood knitted by Elizabeth.

left: Liesl's daughters: Renata in the pink Bonnet (without a flange) and Cecilia in the Ski Bonnet from page 60.

Bunting knitted by Andrea Wong

The Opinionated Knitter

Spun Out #1 , Summer 1981
Elizabeth Zimmermann's Adult Surprise Jacket

Supplying handknitters since 1959

Dear Knitter,

This design has been adapted from the babies' model (Spun Out #1B) by multiple requests. To quote:*"... it looks like nothing on earth when you have finished knitting it. Sew up two shoulder seams and you find the nicest garter-stitch sweater; reversible, with no side or armhole seams and no breaking-off or joining-in of wool."*

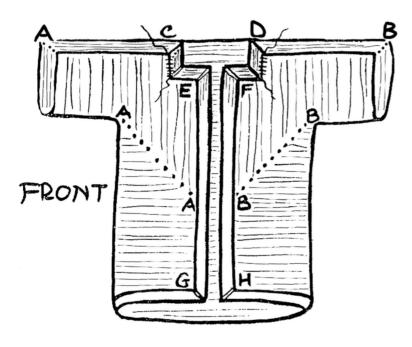

FRONT

Knit it in random stripes, for which you need no directions. As true knitters you have boxes of leftover wools of about the same weight. Mine is made from our 2-ply *Sheepswool*, 2-ply *Unspun Icelandic* and *Canadian Regal* wools with an occasional stripe of some nameless oddment. It weighs exactly 1-1/2 lbs, is 44" around and 26" long.

Experiment with the stripes and add at least one color of each skirt, blouse and turtleneck in your closet; it will then harmonize with everything you wear. I like to change colors on the "right" side, but that is a matter of taste.

DIRECTIONS are governed by [K] -- which is 1/3 of the body-width (**not** circumference). Measure the width of your pet sweater and multiply its inches by **Your Gauge**. Be exact. Divide the result by 3 to obtain **your** Key Number [K]. If the width is 18" or 21" or 24" you are in luck; they divide neatly by 3 and you will need no decimals or fractions or calculators. (For fussy directions on Gauge, see *Knitting Without Tears*, chapter 2. Exact Gauge Is Indispensible.)

With a 24" (or 29") circular needle, CAST ON 9 x [K] and knit back and forth, slipping all first stitches. On the very first row, which is the "wrong" side, mark a stitch at A and B which will be 2 x [K] stitches from either end and work a double-decrease at these points every 2nd row. The ridges of garter-stitch will make a 45° angle (unless you are knitting particularly firmly or loosely) and the random stripes will demark it nobly.

Decrease by Slip 1, K2tog, Psso. **Keep the center stitch constant.** When you have decreased 2 x [K] stitches at each point and are down to 5 x [K] stitches, you are at the underarm.

Now Change Tactics: at the two points (A and B), INCrease 2 stitches every 2nd row by Make 1 on either side of the marked stitch. This will reverse the angle. Keep the center stitch constant. When you are back at the number of stitches you started with (9 x [K]), you are at the neck sides, C and D. Put 3" worth of stitches on pieces of wool at either end and continue working the increasres at A and B until the center-section (between A and B) is 6 x [K] – or twice the wanted width of the sweater. continue on these center stitches only, leaving the end stitches (E - A and F - B) on pieces of wool; they are the center-front stitches.

Work without shaping until the total length from C - G and D - H is about 1" shy of that of your favorite sweater. You are now at the lower corners of the center-front, G and H. NEARLY DONE.

Even though this adult version was not published until well after Newsletter #22, we will include it here as an adjunct to the Baby Surprise Jacket.

SL 1, K2 tog. psso

Now comes a rather awkward part -- which you may like to work on a 40" long circular needle if you have one (I don't, and will struggle with three 24" needles). Knit up one stitch for each ridge along the selvedge G - A just knitted, PLUS the waiting stitches at the front (which were on a piece of wool), PLUS a stitch for each ridge at the neck-front and those 3" worth of stitches at the neck side. Turn and knit back -- repeating the foregoing on the other side. In fact, knit up all stitches in sight as on the odd drawing shown on the next page

M1, K1, M1

Here is the detail that held up this adaptation for years and years*: knit up 1 stitch in each of the cast-on stitches at the lower edge of the sleeve ... from the outside; which is the purl-bump side of Long-tail Casting On. As you, I hope, noticed, I caused you at the very beginning to make the purl-bump side be the "right" side. If you were obedient, you will now reap your reward: garter-stitch knitted up from the purl-bump side of Long Tail Casting-On (and knitted down) is indistinguishable from the rest of the fabric.

Work to wanted sleeve length. No one will guess that the sleeves were knitted down from their lower edges. Cast Off. Sew sleeve-and-shoulder seams. That's it.

Good Knitting -- Elizabeth.

Mark stitches at the inner corners of the neck and at the outer corners of the center-fronts and Purl these single stitches on the "wrong" side. On the right side, work a double-DECrease at the inner corners (perfectionists may like to work this double-decrease by **Slip 2 tog knitwise, K1, pass 2 slipped stitches over**) and a double INCrease at the outer corners. Increase one stitch at the beginning of each of these endless rows to make the neck fit well. After two ridges, make 7 buttonholes, evenly spaced along the appropriate edge. Work 4-5 ridges and cast off in purl on the right side.

From Meg:

Over the years, the greatest difficulty knitters seem to have is keeping the double INCrease and double DECrease diagonals straight and true; it is easy to veer out of line. Think of the dbl-dec as turning **three** stitches into **one**. As soon as you complete your very first dbl-dec, put a coil-less safety pin into the resulting stitch itself (as opposed to a ring marker over the needle). That marked stitch is then the **middle** of the next group of three which will turn into one.

The dbl inc will be easy to see after a few ridges... again, put a coil-less pin into the Important Center Stitch and work a M(ake) 1 on either side of the marked stitch. That marked stitch never varies. The illustration above shows a mirror-image increase which, naturally, is optional. If you use it, you will have to knit into the back of the L side M1 (which will be the first M1 you will meet on your way back) You may prefer to increase by knitting into the running thread... Knitter's choice.

- We recommended that you knit a baby version first (about 3oz Shetland wool and a few evenings of knitting) to give you a rudimentary idea of what you are doing.

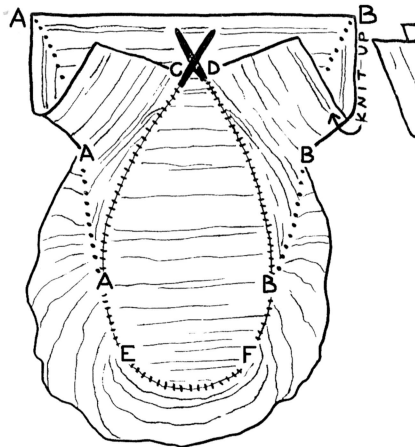

At Knitting Camp '84, Barbro Hardy, Pat Fedders and Sidna Farley said: if you want to make the jacket fit more snugly (a cardigan as opposed to a jacket), you need adjustments to add circumference to the upper sleeve: Cast On **10** x [K] (instead of 9 x [K]. Mark a stitch at A and B **2-1/2** x [K] (instead of 2 x [K]). Decrease down to **6** x [K] (instead of 5 x [K]). Put 4" worth of stitches on threads for neck sides (instead of 3"). These changes put the shoulder seam behind your shoulder, so you can knit up the border around the entire neck and miter the back corners.

Also consider...

- I-Cord trim around all the edges; either a single application, or multiple layers.

- If the jacket is knitted with wool heavier than Shetland, a hood is a handsome addition; see general instructions for the Tomten jacket hood on page 42

- Before uniting the shoulders, have some fun by tossing it to someone (knitter or not) and challenge them to fold that amorphous bit of knitting into a sweater.

- **Elizabeth's After-Thought-Pockets** may be added, as shown on page 116 (barely visible): try on the sweater and note where your hand wants to go into a pocket. Mark the center-stitch of the proposed pocket and find the mirror-image stitch on the other side. Snip half of the marked stitch and ravel stitches in either direction until the opening is just wide enough to admit your hand. Pick up the lower stitches and cast them off (in I-Cord if you like). Pick up the top stitches and begin to work the pocket back and forth: first a few ridges of garter-stitch, then switch to stocking stitch for a smooth lining, but keep the first and last 5 stitches in garter-stitch so they will lie flat as you stitch down the edges later. After about two inches straight, begin to increase at the beginning of the row every 3rd ridge until the pocket is nice and wide, then continue straight to wanted depth. Cast Off. Stitch down the three sides.

Elizabeth designed the *Baby Surprise Jacket* in 1968 and it remains very popular. She resisted designing an Adult version because the formula resulted in elbow-length sleeves and she disliked the appearance of knitting-up from the outline-stitch-side of Long Tail Casting On. Serendipitously, while knitting her magical Garter-Stitch Heart design, she realized that if stitches are knitted up from the "wrong", or purl-bump side, the join is undetectable.

Since then, Carol Anderson (of *Cottage Creations* fame) had an inspiration to Cast On **Invisibly.** You then have raw stitches around the cuff and can easily lengthen the sleeves. To keep the shoulder seam firm, you may cast on the first and last bits (2 x [K]) Invisibly, and use Long-Tail Cast On for the middle stitches.

Either of the above two options works very well.

Elizabeth writes:

One of my greatest comforts and conveniences in daily life is to have plenty of spectacles. I don't mean eyeglasses, for which one has to go to the eye-man and pay a fortune for and weep salt tears over when they drop and break. I mean spectacles, which you buy at any self-respecting five-and-dime, unless you live in a pettifogging State which meddles in what is none of its business and forbids their free sale and purchase.

When I got to be about fifty, the Telephone Company started to cut down drastically on the quality of the printing in its books. They also changed the typeface so that numbers began to look alike, especially the 6s, 8s and 3s. I cast my mind back to the memory of my old father at the same age. He bought steel-rimmed spectacles at Woolworths. My mother used to scold him, saying he would ruin his eyesight, and why didn't he wear proper glasses from Dr. Johnson.

Following his example, then, I explored the nearest variety store, and sure enough there was a thriving spectacles-counter with a printed card on how to pick out the right strength.

I fooled around with different models and different potencies -- rather tricky, because when you have found the kind that suits you, you have to take them off to see what number they are, and then you haven't got them on and cannot read the number. I settled on #18 as enabling me most effectively to read something held 14 inches away from my nose, and invested in two models: an owlish pair which the salesgirl said were for men, and a very twee pair of just the lower halves, rimmed in pale grey.

They lasted a long time. The owlish pair is still around, for emergencies, its earpieces firmly tied with string. The grey half-glasses were inadvertently left in Hatchards, on Piccadilly

(showing off again, but true). When I discovered their loss, halfway to somewhere else in a plane, I did not gasp and go through a lot of fuss having them sent after me and mailing small amounts of foreign currency about Europe. I reached into my knitting bag and extracted an identical pair – #18 – cleverly brought with me for just such an occasion, and abandoned the original pair to their surely happy fate. Occasionally I think about them. I imagine they spent some time in Hatchard's Lost-and-Found (English shops are notoriously honest) and then perhaps at the Christmas Party, Mr Hatchard organized a basket of all the unclaimed items and somebody fished them out ... a rare and expensive pair of foreign spectacles ... and wears them carefully and contentedly to this day. If they need #18 that is, and have no superstitions about ruining their eyes.

Dozens of pairs have I bought since then. I spend no frustrating hours hunting when a pair is mislaid; I just grab the nearest of many other pairs, confident that the lost ones will turn up. They nearly always do, and if they don't what would have been the use of keeping on looking for them? Lost and Gone Forever, they are.

And don't think I've not had to stand up to mockery and predictions of eye-ruin and blindness. It's well over ten years now and I'm still wearing #18s, while many of the mockers are eternally graduating to new and stronger lenses.

One further advantage, which I found out by pure chance: when you are in a rage, it is MOST effective to fling your spectacles across the room ... they've never broken on me yet, and it stops acrimonious argument in its tracks.

Elizabeth Zimmermann

I also prefer winters to some other seasons I could name. So pretty and clean and spare. And plenty of time for, and call for, knitting.

No book #3 is contemplated. But if my heirs and assigns one day want to gather up a selection of Wool Gathering s for this purpose I shall bless them. The new one next month is on Fair Isles. Great fun.

Good Knitting.

Elizabeth.

The Opinionated Knitter

(continued from page 91)

The second schoolhouse will probably be our last, anyway.

The first schoolhouse was bought over 14 years ago and we love it dearly; the second is our ace-in-the-hole, to be saved for our old age.

Studying a grid-like inch-to-the-mile map of our area one day, I found a piece of road with a hiccup in it and, curious, I guided us in the direction of this diversion one day when we were roaming around. The road jiggled because it went up over a hill – which is most unusual in our part of the state – and there, almost at the top, was a white clapboard schoolhouse with what looked like a happy family living in it and little kids playing around. Good, I thought, another schoolhouse family; what a beauty theirs is. Right at the schoolhouse itself a road turned East to run along the hill and our breath was taken away. There to the South the flat sand-country spread out, interrupted only occasionally by a low hill or so (we call them "Bluffs") but otherwise flat as a pancake.

We stopped next to a white farmhouse to gaze our fill. Do you think he'd sell a couple acres? someone said. Hoo boy, what a view; what a place to live. Take it easy, someone else said, we've just bought a schoolhouse, haven't we? What'd we do with another? We heaved a collective sigh, started the engine, drove on and forgot. In my case, for "forgot", read "almost forgot".

One day, as I was studying the Record, the magic word AUCTION caught my eye. Three schoolhouses were to be bid on and one of them was the Cary Bluff Schoolhouse.

Cary Bluff was that hill on which the road had hiccupped. Could it be possible? I am a canny old woman when big things are at stake. I didn't immediately holler, "Auction" at the top of my voice; I've found that this word brings unfavorable, not to say scornful, reaction from my nearest and dearest. I lay very low until next weekend, when we had occasion to drive around on Saturday afternoon. Quite casually I said that there were some pretty roads to the Northwest and climbed into the car with the inch-to-the-mile maps. With these I carefully steered our driver in the direction of the three schoolhouses, which I had of course thoroughly researched in the meantime. As we came upon the first one I said, my gosh this must be the one that was advertised for sale, but of course it's right on the highway let's go and see the others they're not far. The second one was brick and had to be moved. Let's try the third one; I believe it's on Cary Bluff.

It was looking its best on that lovely late-summer day. It was closed and deserted (I found out later that the "family" had been the school cleaner and her kids.) The view was lovelier than ever; we stopped the car and gazed at it. Oh well, I said, city people will prolly (sic) come to the auction and bid to hell and gone. We drove on. The Schoolhouse was not referred to again.

As the auction day approached I laid my plans. By some clever arranging on the part of the gods, auction day and opening day of duck hunting season were one and the same. The Old Man is never quite sane in hunting season. Gee, I'd like to go to that schoolhouse auction, I said, how much do you think it'll fetch? Whyntcha go? he said, of course I'll be out after ducks. Huck! went my heart. Well I might, I said. I could even bid on it for fun. How high would you go, just for kicks? We-ell, twenny-five hundred to three thousand, he said.

Wow! I'd made it!

E l i z a b e t h   Z i m m e r m a n n

Of course Rich People might be there. I checked all the savings-books and mustered another 300 bucks of my own. These I metaphorically pinned to my corset-cover when I set off on Saturday, October 5th; a perfect Fall day, clear and still.

Loudly I sang to myself as I bowled along. Auctions are the breath of life to me and I don't get nearly enough of them. Mostly I bid on beat-up apple boxes or bins full of miscellaneous junk. Very small beer, but to me, intoxicating. The things I like are usually the worthless items which are sold off first. But today I was after bigger game – the schoolhouses themselves would doubtless be put up last.

The auction was being held at another small one-room schoolhouse and I mingled with the throng, trying not to look as foreign as I felt, knowing nobody but rather hoping that people who didn't know me would think there were others who did. I get these vain hopes when I am solitary in a group, and there's not a thing I can do about it.

The auctioneer materialized, and the clerk with his canvas apron, and the first thing the auctioneer said was that since there was a party interested in the schoolhouses who didn't have much time, these would be sold first. He can't mean me, I thought, and I was right; it was a buncha of guys from Chicago. Alas, I thought, for the 3300 bucks.

The two smaller schoolhouses were sold first and such was my excitement that I didn't even notice what for.

Then, with insouciance, I moved back and leaned against a fence with no one in front of me, so the auctioneer would easily see me as I casually laid a finger to my nose or wiggled my ears at him. Just like a real auction, my dears. I felt wonderful.

Things started slowly, and at about $500 I began to put in my 5¢ worth from time to time. At $900 things changed. All the bidders except me and the guys from Chicago dropped out and damme if those Chicagoans didn't cost me eight hundred and fifty dollars. But at seventeen-fifty they gave up and the schoolhouse was mine.

I made a down-payment, signed something, got the key and floated out of there on the wings of a dove. I made a slight detour on my way home to look at our new possession – fairer than the dreams of avarice, it was – and arrived back just ahead of the duck-hunters, who had had their limit I'm happy to say, it having been a good day all around. I handed the Old Man the key, metaphorically popped my 300 back in the savings accounts and from that day on we have been entitled to call ourselves collectors of schoolhouses.

That building, renovated and bristling with offices, warehouses, studios and photo-voltaic arrays, has become Schoolhouse Press.

WOOL GATHERING from Meg Swansen

issue #62 March, 2000

Dear Knitter,

On November 30th, '99 my mother, died. We told very few people -- hardly able to believe it ourselves -- and Amy Detjen waited a few days before releasing the information to knitters via Knit-U on the internet.

News travels at unbelievable speed these days and within a few hours I received a phone call from the *New York Times*. Elizabeth's obituary and photograph were printed in the following Sunday edition and the announcement was subsequently picked up by scores of newspapers around the US, which inspired follow-up editorials and letters-to-the-editor.

National Public Radio telephoned for an interview the following day and I spoke to Noah Adams on *All Things Considered*. A few hours later I talked about my mother to Mary Lou Finley on *As It Happens* on CBC public radio in Toronto.

For weeks the incoming mail was a surreal mixture of wool orders, festive holiday greetings and condolence cards.

The fact that my mother's death preceded by four days the fourth anniversary of my husband's death, made it particularly poignant.

I remain convinced that my family and I were able to wade through the ensuing weeks by dint of the loving thoughts, e-mail, flowers, phone calls, letters and cards from knitters around the world. All of the above are forms of prayer and the support they provided is undeniable. Every letter and note has been preserved.

We had thought we were fully aware of Elizabeth's popularity among knitters. Her books and video sales plus the frequent and generous acknowledgements of her influence by many other designers and magazines, bespoke a wide array of followers. But we far underestimated the depth and breadth of her impact upon the knitting world and we remain a bit stunned by the realization that our wife, mother, grandmother and great-grandmother was also a Knitting Mother to such a vast number of people.

This memorial issue is a collection of photographs and comments from knitters.

WOOL GATHERING

Elizabeth Zimmermann
1910-1999

These final pages are from *Wool Gathering #62.*

Wool Gathering appears in March & September. $4 each, or by subscription: 3 years (6 issues) $20.00; overseas Air Mail, $25.00   © 2000 Schoolhouse Press. All rights reserved.
The number after your name on the address label is the final WG in your subscription.
Published by **Schoolhouse Press, 6899 Cary Bluff, Pittsville, WI 54466**
phone: (715) 884-2799   fax: (715) 884-2829   order line: (800) YOU-KNIT
Founded in 1959 by Elizabeth Zimmermann

Kaffe Fassett telephoned CBC radio from London "to pay homage to Elizabeth, who is one of the most extraordinary influences in my life." They had corresponded for years and in her initial letter to Kaffe, Elizabeth wrote, "... go out and buy a circular needle; it will change your life." Kaffe said, "...so I did ... and it did!"

Here are excerpts from some of the letters we received:

"Not only was she a leading light for the liberation of knitters, she was and still is, a leading light for living."

"She is one of the persons whose spirit transcends time and space and touch all who come to her..."

"Isn't it wonderful to sit down with EZ's storytelling when you are otherwise inclined to pop another Prozac?"

"*Knitting Without Tears* was the first knitting book I ever picked up that was truly instructional and not just a compilation of patterns to follow."

"For me, it was the first time I'd been exposed to knitting theory and the first time a knitting-book author had encouraged readers not only to alter patterns to their own taste and needs, but to bravely sally forth and dare to think up designs on their own."

"I feel as though I have lost a member of my own family."

"Not only did she encourage and teach us to knit, but her gentle graciousness, generosity and humor were a lovely inspiration of how to live our lives."

"She was a hero to me both as a designer and a philosopher and I love the grace and confidence with which she wrote. She inspired the person as well as the knitter in me."

"I am one of the multitude of women who knit because of Elizabeth."

"I wonder if she had any idea how influential she was as a knitting-attitude-adjuster. What a unique woman -- a breath of Spring air, a hug of encouragement, an inspiration for creativity."

"I wept when I read of Elizabeth's passing."

"Elizabeth in particular gave me a sense of being able to believe that most things in knitting -- and life too -- happen in ways that are open to an inquiring brain. Perhaps that sounds too dramatic, but I know that what I learned from her changed me for the better in every way I can understand it."

"She has inspired me, given me freedom to create and to be in control of much more that just my knitting."

"When I found Elizabeth, knitting stopped being a hobby and became a way of life."

"I am a knitwear designer, because of Elizabeth Zimmermann. It's that simple. ... I am a fuller, more creative, and more confident person, because of her."

"I know that any success I have had as a designer, and the fact that I AM a designer is because of her."

"Very simply put, Elizabeth Zimmermann changed my knitting life."

"I am crying now as I type; I feel like I lost my own mother. And in a way I have. Knitting is a sisterhood and Elizabeth was our mentor, our sister, our mother, our friend."

"Elizabeth was brilliant and gifted and physically beautiful, even into old age, because she had a radiant soul .... I can't believe I'm sitting at my computer crying for a woman I've never met, but that's the effect your mother had on all of us. She was, quite simply, the Knitting Goddess and she always will be."

"EZ is an icon to the knitting community and her spirit and large body of work will live on inspiring too many to count."

"I first read Knitting Without Tears in 1993. It was, and remains, a revelation. I was a blind follower of knitting patterns until just a few years ago, and now, EZ's example is a constant inspiration."

"She brought laughter into my knitting and encouraged me to continue what was a very solitary occupation."

"I have no doubt she is teaching St Peter to knit while he is on gate duty!"

"... then came Elizabeth and I now knit from my heart and my head; no more 'blind following' for me!"

"A friend went to a workshop in the Adirondacks and came back full of this teacher who arrived on the back of a *motorcycle* all the way from Wisconsin!"

"I've loved Elizabeth for so long and thought that she was truly my guardian angel."

"I never met Elizabeth Zimmermann, but she was one of my dearest knitting mentors and friends."

"I learned to knit before she came into my life, but she taught me to ENJOY knitting and to take pride in my work."

"Tears of gratitude that we all had an opportunity to experience the genius of Elizabeth Zimmermann in her writings, workshops and videos."

"I treasure her little notes to me and a swatch she knitted for me when I couldn't understand Short Rows. She told me to donate a sum to charity for her time ... which I did."

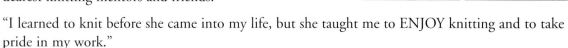

Elizabeth Zimmermann

1964, Chris on the left.

"Elizabeth was a blessing ... I feel as if I knew her and she has been in my heart for 25 years."

"*Knitting Without Tears* got me started as a thinking knitter at the very beginning of my knitting career ... she had such a profound effect on me."

"She's my Knitting Guru. I've learned so much from her, not only about knitting but about how to live your life."

"My favorite image is of her, behind Gaffer on the motorcycle, knitting away."

"Our local contingent of Old Knitting Hippies has decided that EZ was the Jerry Garcia of knitting: jolly, kind, unconventional, endlessly creative, often quoted and much loved by countless people."

"Once I tried EPS I was on my way, not knowing that that book would break the ground for me to start designing for magazines."

"... and what a brilliant artist she was. Seeing her drawings and paintings in her books is another form of inspiration. EZ was talented in so many ways."

"EZ's Pelerine suddenly has great significance. I feel all warm and cozy with it wrapped around my shoulders and I feel the Guardian Angel of Knitting smiling with approval every time I wear it. Generations from now, her books and videos will still be showing the way."

"At first, it took a little time for me to 'get' what she was saying, but once I did - watch out! Here was someone actually encouraging me to question a pattern ... to look for an easier way ... to truly understand that what my fingers were doing was not merely mechanical but magical."

"I thought of her only a few weeks prior to her death when I had all my grade-3 boys gathered tightly around me as they took their first stitches on a garter stitch square."

"Elizabeth has been my knitting buddy for over 25 years ... a welcomed friend in my home and heart."

124

Betty Lloyd-Jones, about 1930.

"...no more a blind follower. And now feel such a great loss. Just finished my third of six Surprise Jackets. Am I a fan? You betcha."

"With gratitude to EZ for her priceless legacy."

"Elizabeth's own life seems to be proof that we should do what we love and success will follow. Thank you for enriching my life."

"...but isn't that the sign of a great artist - they have the ability to exact a change in you no matter how great the physical or temporal distance?"

"Young knitters as yet unborn, will be taught their craft by EZ, I am sure."

"I just 'discovered' EZ this year but she has changed my knitting life. ...I'm grateful for having been touched by such an angel."

"The New York Times is noted for its short obituaries, so the length of EZ's says a lot about her importance."

"I already knew how to knit but I became a Knitter when I first read EZ and had The Knitter's Epiphany!

"I can't get further than thinking that my life would have been entirely different without Elizabeth. Everywhere I look there are people I know because of knitting. And for me knitting began with Elizabeth."

"I am convinced that the knitting world as we know it now wouldn't have existed, had she not spurred so many of us on. Her techniques revolutionized knitting the way no one else had done..."

"I always thought of your mom as a relative of mine, too... she was my idol."

"Someone recommended "Knitting Without Tears" to me and it changed my knitting life...."

"Knitting in the round! No more putzy seams to sew? I was in HEAVEN! ...If it wasn't for EZ, I probably would have given up on knitting."

In her sailboat on the Chiemsee in Bavaria, 1934

Elizabeth Zimmermann

"I am filled with gratitude, appreciation, admiration, affection, awe, joy ... and I just smile when I think of Elizabeth."

"Death cannot diminish her vibrancy and vitality which shines through her books and videos."

"I always recommend *'Knitting Without Tears'* to people who need to loosen up about knitting ..."

"I don't know how many times I would put her tapes in the VCR just to have her there in the room to listen to - especially when things weren't going so well in my own life. And how she still makes me laugh when she dances a little jig in those enormous bear-paw slippers at the end of *Knitting Glossary* video!"

"My first thought was a quote from Obi Wan Kenobi ... 'I sense a great disturbance in the force, as though a million voices had cried out in pain.' I feel that Elizabeth was THE knitting force of her time."

"Every night I read a little dab of *Knitter's Almanac*. It is even better the 103rd time through."

"What a wonderful writer she was. Whenever I have a knitting question my first thought is, 'what does EZ have to say?'"

"I know she was a great knitter, but the person who shines through those four books was a wonderful, warm woman. Not to mention beautiful!"

"I often have Elizabeth to tea by putting in a tape and knitting as Meg and Elizabeth banter. "

"I just wanted to share my joy over the EZ books that I am now marinating in each night. What treasures!"

"The greatest thing EZ gave me was freedom to be creative, not only in my knitting but in anything I want to do ... and this includes going back to college at age 50+."

"Right hand over my heart and genuflect toward WI - thank you, EZ for being the soothing voice in the night during a time of emotional trial."

1958 - leaning on a bright-red Borgward; her Knitted Car (paid for entirely with money she earned by knitting.)

Elizabeth's Striped Tams:

A number of years ago Elizabeth tried to think of a productive way to use up her growing collection of little wool oddments that accumulated so quickly and continuously. She pounced upon the idea of knitting a series of striped tam o'shanters and began by separating the leftovers (all being more or less the same weight) into two baskets, which she placed on either side of her. One basket held bits of dark colors, the other contained all lighter shades.

The tams were comprised of single-round-stripes of dark and light colors. At the end of each round, EZ blindly reached into each container alternately, to pull out the next color. She was not permitted (by herself) to exchange any color; it HAD to be the first one she touched. When the round was completed, the color was then taken out of the rotation.

She had a wonderful time, made dozens of tams (all of which were subsequently given away), combined colors that she never would have dreamed of putting together in cold blood and made productive use of all those small bits of wool that you cannot quite bring yourself to throw away.

Here is a note and a poem Elizabeth sent to Barbara Carlson, *"From an old musical from my youth called 'Nymph Errant':*

in NYC

Experiment! Make it your motto day and night.
Experiment! And it can lead you to the light.
The apple on the top of the tree
Is never too hard to achieve,
So take an example from Eve,
Experiment!
Be curious, though interfering friends may frown,
Get furious at all attempts to hold you down.
If this advice you only employ
The future can bring to you
infinite joy
And merriment.
Experiment
And you'll see."

"...she said at my first Camp, 'Don't worry, lovey, I'll teach you to knit.' I bought my first VCR only because her TV tapes were finally available to us."

"EZ rocks!"

"Where would knitting be without Elizabeth?"

"... she gave us 'permission' to use our own minds - what a gift. I remember asking her to sign my *Knitting Workshop*. I apologized for asking and her reply was, 'My dear, whoever would have thought that I would have written a book?'"

"Beyond the knitting is the personal growth and confidence that is felt by those that have followed the path cleared by both of you. We are not entangled by cumbersome directions, but can think on our own."

"Like so many knitters, I feel that my life and work have been greatly enhanced by Elizabeth's gentle, practical and always inquisitive forays into knitting."

"I am a knitter because of Elizabeth. Only if J.R.R. Tolkien had been a knitter could such enchanting books as hers have been written by anyone else."

"I bought my first copy of *Knitting Without Tears* at a bookstore close-out because it was cheap. I had no idea of the impact that that book would have on my life."

Photograph by Walter Sheffer for *Knitting Without Tears*. Elizabeth had planned the shot to show her knitting on the sleeve of the sweater she was wearing ... but on the dust jacket, Scribner's cropped the photo just above her hands.

"Elizabeth and her husband came to SOAR ... I was prepared to be awestruck, but they were so kind and so obviously in deep love; how could anyone be anything but charmed..."

age 17, with her cat, Nouncer

How heartening it is that Elizabeth was recognized for her contributions to knitting (and writing) during her lifetime. She derived enormous satisfaction from knowing that her approach had worked its way so solidly into the knitting language.

Many decades ago, as a diversion and a game, my mother and four of her close friends each wrote their own epitaphs. Ruth Hainer wrote, "Ruth Cast Off". My mother wrote:

me and ma

> *Elizabeth was sitting,*
> *Cat on lap.*
> *She put down her knitting and*
> *Took a nap.*

E l i z a b e t h   Z i m m e r m a n n